THE WALL STREET JOURNAL.

PERSONAL FINANCE WORKBOOK

OTHER BOOKS BY JEFF D. OPDYKE AND
THE WALL STREET JOURNAL

The Wall Street Journal. Guide to the Business of Life
Nancy Keates

The Wall Street Journal. Complete Money & Investing Guidebook
Dave Kansas

The Wall Street Journal. Complete Personal Finance Guidebook
Jeff D. Opdyke

Love and Money: A Life Guide to Financial Success
Jeff D. Opdyke

THE WALL STREET JOURNAL.

PERSONAL FINANCE WORKBOOK

JEFF D. OPDYKE

THREE RIVERS PRESS
NEW YORK

Published in the United States by Three Rivers Press, an imprint of the Crown Publishing Group, a division of Random House, Inc., New York.
www.crownpublishing.com

Library of Congress Cataloging-in-Publication Data is available upon request.

ISBN-13: 978-0-307-33601-9
ISBN-10: 0-307-33601-8

Printed in the United States of America

Design by Mauna Eichner and Lee Fukui

10 9 8 7 6 5

First Edition

CONTENTS

INTRODUCTION 1

PART I
BUILDING YOUR FINANCIAL BASE

CHAPTER 1 **BUDGETING** 7

The Personal Budget 9
The Spending Plan 12
Pay Yourself First 20
Emergency Savings 25
The Annual Budget 27

CHAPTER 2 **BANKING: CHECKING, SAVINGS, AND CERTIFICATES OF DEPOSIT** 35

Checking Accounts 36
Certificates of Deposit—
and When Breaking One Makes Sense 40
Building a CD Ladder 47

CHAPTER 3 PLANNING: PREPARING FOR THE WORST 49

Insurance 49
Do I Need Insurance? 50
How Much Insurance Do I Need? 52

CHAPTER 4 BORROWING: ACCUMULATING AND MANAGING DEBT 61

Warning Signs You Carry Too Much Debt 62
Is Your Debt Too High? 63
Paying Down Debt 64
Buying a Home 68
Renting Versus Buying: Weighing the Trade-Offs 69
How Much Can You Afford? 72
Shopping for a Loan 76
Tax Savings 78
Calculating the Equity in Your Home 79
To Refinance or Not 81
The Old College Try: Saving for a Child's Education 81
How Much to Save? 86
Buying a Car 92
The Ins and Outs of Auto Leases 95
Turning a Money Factor into an Interest Rate 99
Comparing Leases 100

CHAPTER 5 BE PREPARED—IT'S NOT JUST A MOTTO FOR THE BOY SCOUTS 103

The Wallet Register 103
Financial Accounts 104
Safe-Deposit Boxes 106

PART II
BUILDING YOUR ASSETS

CHAPTER 6 INVESTING 117

Determining Your Net Worth 118
Rating Your Tolerance for Risk 120
Short Term? Long Term? Something in Between? 122
Compounding: The Most Powerful Force in the Universe 127
First Things First 128
Brokerage-Firm Basics 129
Wall Street in Words and Formulas 132
Calculating Your Rate of Return 135
Index Investing: No Effort Required 138
Exchange-Traded Funds: Minimal Effort Required 139
Dollar-Cost Averaging 140

CHAPTER 7 RETIREMENT PLANNING: FEATHERING THE NEST EGG 145

How Much Will I Need in Retirement? 145
Asset Allocation: Rocket Science for Beginners 153
Asset Allocation Models 154
Where Do I Invest? 156
What Might a Diversified Portfolio Look Like? 160
Company Stock: Buy, Sell, or Hold? 162
The ABCs of IRAs 162
Annuities: Great for Some; Lousy for Many 164
Which Annuity Is Right for Me? 168
A Taxing Matter 169

CONCLUSION 171

Index 173

THE WALL STREET JOURNAL.

PERSONAL FINANCE WORKBOOK

INTRODUCTION

The simple fact about personal finance is that managing your money requires a bit of math. Sorry.

In truth, most of the math is easy and obvious, though some of it can seem complex when you must make comparisons between, say, buying a car and taking the rebate or the 0% financing, or leasing the vehicle instead. With some of it, like gauging your potential financial needs for retirement or gauging the costs of college eighteen years from now—well, it's sometimes hard to even know where to begin.

Thus, this workbook.

These pages are designed to complement a companion book, *The Wall Street Journal Complete Personal Finance Guidebook,* a thorough primer for understanding and taking control of every aspect of your personal financial life. That said, this workbook is written to stand on its own for those who already have a working knowledge of personal finance and just want a resource to help calculate, for instance, when it makes sense to refinance your home or how to comparison-shop for the best mortgage. Along with various worksheets and formulas designed to make the math part of personal finance easier, a variety of tips are interspersed throughout to help you make better decisions when spending, saving, and investing your limited resources. Also, given that we live in the Internet age, interactive versions of the worksheets can be found online at www.WSJ.com/BookTools.

This workbook is divided into two broad sections: "Building Your Financial Base" and "Building Your Assets." The first section tackles what we'll call domestic finance—all that money stuff that happens in the home: creating a budget, balancing a checkbook, managing your debt, and protecting your family's assets with life insurance. In that section you'll also find help planning for college and planning for the worst—the possibility that bad things happen that require you to tap into emergency savings or which demand you produce a full and immediate accounting of the possessions in your home. You'll also learn how to determine in your situation the smartest method for acquiring a car.

The second section pulls apart what you need to know about investing, everything from buying stocks through a brokerage firm to determining the right type of annuity for you and your family. In between you'll find worksheets that will help you gauge your own tolerance for risk, and a rundown of the terms and formulas that Wall Street employs. The "Building Your Assets" section is largely structured around putting together a well-diversified portfolio in your retirement savings accounts, since preparing for retirement is the most significant investment purpose most readers will have.

To paraphrase Woody Allen's famous claim that 90% of success is just showing up: 90% of financial success is just trying. You don't need to be a certified financial planner; you don't need to be a chartered financial analyst. You don't need to be a mutual-fund portfolio manager or a Wall Street investment banker. You don't even need a degree in finance to manage your own money.

All you need you already have: a desire to know and a workbook to lead the way.

Oh, and of course, a little math, which we're going to help you with.

PART I

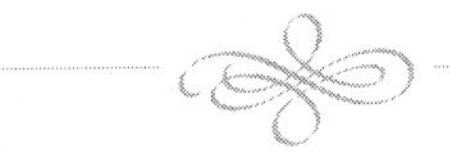

BUILDING YOUR FINANCIAL BASE

Pyramids all start the same: a solid base on which to build the rest of the structure. Personal finance is no different.

Sure, you can start at the top, throwing your money into investments like stocks and bonds and annuities, hoping that will turn a few dollars into a fortune so large you don't need to worry about all those niggling financial matters like balancing your checkbook and saving. Or you wake up from the dream and start at the beginning. Even the superwealthy plan their finances and pay attention to the basics. That's how many of them became rich in the first place.

Neither wealth, however you define that, nor financial security happens overnight. Yes, there are a number of people who win lotteries and suddenly come into instant riches. And many of them end up spending or wasting most of their winnings; some even end up in bankruptcy court. For you see, financial success has nothing to do with having a lot of money; it's about having a lot of success managing the money you do have. You can make $100,000 a year and live paycheck to paycheck and on the brink of insolvency because you can't manage your spending and you have no idea how to save (and many, many people are in this position). Similarly, you can earn $40,000 and know without question that you are financially secure and solvent, and that you have adequate savings to help cover a rainy day as well as your retirement some day (and there are many, many people in this position, too).

Those who know success built a solid base early on. And they know that base begins with that most dreaded of words in personal finance: *budget.*

CHAPTER 1

BUDGETING

Have you ever driven from Mount Sterling, Utah, to Dixville Notch, New Hampshire? Do you even know how to begin planning that route? If you're fairly fluent with the points on a compass, you could probably wind your way out of the Wasatch Mountains and head in the general direction of the East Coast, but you'd likely have a challenging time with the finer points of efficiently finding your way to Dixville Notch in the far northern tip of New Hampshire.

A road map would offer immense utility.

In many ways, budgeting is the roadmap to your finances. After all, moving in generally the right direction is fairly easy, but it doesn't necessarily get you to where you think you're going. You know you have to set aside enough money from each paycheck to pay the bills, and you know you're supposed to save something, if you can, for that proverbial rainy day. For a lot of people, that defines the extent of their budgeting—spend what you need; save what you can.

Imagine, though, having a benevolent guide to steer your path, to show you where you're spending. You'd have a better grasp of the costs that are necessary in your life, and those that are extraneous. Thus informed, you'd be prepared to make smarter decisions on spending and saving. That doesn't mean you'd be tethered to a budget that sapped the fun from your days and nights. Rather, you'd be empowered to decide for yourself what you want to spend your money on. It may be that you want to spend $3,000 on a vacation to Cairo instead of fund an individual retirement account, and that's fine. But your problem is you can't spare the cash because your expenses never leave anything but pocket change at the end of every month.

With a plan, however, you might quickly find that many of the daily expenses you have in life aren't necessary, and that with a little jiggering you can alter your monthly spending so that you can actually save for what you want: that trip—or the money to fund that IRA, or cover the down payment on a new car, or whatever want sits atop your wish list.

The key to all of this and more is your budget.

Of course, for many people the word *budget* immediately conjures up disagreeable images of a binding straightjacket—a confining document that tells you what you can and can't spend.

Budgets don't have to be that way. Budgets don't even have to be budgets. You can think of them, instead, as spending plans. Though it sounds like so much semantics, budgets and spending plans are different if only because of the psychological reaction they each illicit. Where budgets bespeak confinement, spending plans epitomize freedom because they allow you to make the decisions on how you want to spend or save your money. Here's why the psychological impact of a spending plan is relevant: Money is as much about psychology as it is about finance. How you think about money and the lessons you've learned about money through the years—from parents, in particular—shape the way you spend and save, often without your even realizing it. By using a different type of budgeting system, a spending plan, you regain control psychologically, often the trick many people need to better live within their means.

Essentially, a spending plan works by matching your known income to your necessary expenses each month. Then, the plan allows you to resolve how you want to distribute any excess cash that remains—your discretionary income. You can choose to pay down your credit card or car note, erasing your debt quicker. You can choose to put that money toward a vacation, a new washing machine, a fancy meal at a restaurant with your significant other. You can opt to bury it in the backyard, buy shares of a mutual fund, open a Roth IRA, or fund a college savings account for your child. Basically, you can do whatever you want with your money because you're the one calling the shots.

That might not seem like such a huge leap forward in the art of budgeting, but, again, money is often a psychological and emotional game. If a spending plan leaves you feeling in charge of your money, while a budget leaves you feeling like a slave to your money, chances are very good that the spending plan survives to help you achieve financial success, while a budget is exiled to the garbage bin, never to help you achieve much of anything.

Ultimately, a personal budget and a spending plan accomplish the same goal—providing a framework for sensible spending and healthy saving. In order to see that, and to build the financial foundation you need so that you can better understand the way your money flows through your life, starting off with a personal budget and working your way up to a spending plan is a solid idea.

THE PERSONAL BUDGET

You don't have to rush into a full-blown, detailed spending plan immediately if the thought of trying to wrap your arms around all of your monthly finances is intimidating. Instead, this personal budget allows you to set an expected spending limit in various broad categories at the start of the month, and then at the end of the month you compare your actual costs with your budgeted costs. Seeing those differences month in and month out gives you a clearer understanding of where you're really spending your money, knowledge that ultimately will allow you to scale back spending on what you determine is wasteful or unnecessary, and beef up your outlays in those categories that are more meaningful to your life.

More important, the personal budget will reveal—before your spending begins for the month—whether your expectations exceed your bankroll. If they do, you'll need to recalibrate your expected spending to match your expected income, otherwise you'll be the embodiment of "living beyond your means," an assured path to financial ruin if the trend persists.

Come month's end, you have a few tasks: foremost, if your spending has exceeded your income, you need to examine those categories where you overspent and ask yourself what happened. If over several months you see that you consistently overspend in certain categories, the problem could be that you are underestimating how important these areas are to your lifestyle. Basically, you're underbudgeting and will need to readjust. Or it could be that you're not exercising enough self-restraint in your discretionary spending, something that you must address, because a certain amount of discipline is a key component for anyone who wants to succeed with their finances. At some point, you have to be accountable to yourself.

In similar fashion, you should discipline yourself to examine your personal budget every month, looking for categories where you not only exceed your anticipated expenses, but also those where you overbudgeted. Then you can effectively shift your spending away from categories that have proven to be less important to you than you imagine, and into those categories where you are actually spending your dollars.

BUILDING A PERSONAL BUDGET

- First, make several copies of this worksheet so that you have a blank one handy each month.
- Start each month by estimating your income and expenses in each of the various categories. With certain expenses, such as a car payment or rent, this will be easy. With other expenses, such as food and entertainment, it's more of an educated guess.
- During the month, save all of your receipts, or keep a running tab of your costs in each category on a separate sheet of paper.
- At the end of the month, tally up your actual costs and compare them to your expected costs.
- In the first three months, the goal of this exercise is to see where you're over- or underbudgeting so that you gain a better feel for the true expenses you have in life. After the first few months, the purpose of this exercise shifts to encourage you to think at the beginning of each month about how you want to allocate your cash. If you know, for instance, that you would like to replace your aging DVD player, you will have an intimate enough understanding of your budget to cut back on items such as meals out, entertainment, or clothing expenses.
- Remember: This is a simplified, down-and-dirty version of the more detailed Spending Plan. When you decide to move up to the Spending Plan, your entries here can be transferred directly across.

Income	**Budget**	**Actual**	**Difference**
Income #1	$ ________	$ ________	$ ________
Income #2	$ ________	$ ________	$ ________
Income #3	$ ________	$ ________	$ ________
Other	$ ________	$ ________	$ ________
Other	$ ________	$ ________	$ ________
Total Monthly Income	$ ________	$ ________	$ ________

Expenses	**Budget**	**Actual**	**Difference**
Fixed Expenses			
Rent/Mortgage	$ ________	$ ________	$ ________
Home owner's/renter's insurance	$ ________	$ ________	$ ________
Car payment	$ ________	$ ________	$ ________
Car insurance	$ ________	$ ________	$ ________
Life/health insurance	$ ________	$ ________	$ ________
School tuition/child care	$ ________	$ ________	$ ________
Internet service	$ ________	$ ________	$ ________
Savings (pay yourself first)	$ ________	$ ________	$ ________
Credit-card payment	$ ________	$ ________	$ ________
Fixed Expenses Subtotal	$ ________	$ ________	$ ________
Nonfixed Expenses			
Groceries	$ ________	$ ________	$ ________

Expenses	Budget	Actual	Difference
Nonfixed Expenses *(continued)*			
Meals out	$	$	$
Utilities/water/sewage	$	$	$
Cable/satellite TV	$	$	$
Phone/long distance	$	$	$
Cell phone	$	$	$
Medical expenses	$	$	$
Nonfixed Expenses Subtotal	$	$	$
Transportation			
Gasoline	$	$	$
Bus/subway/ferry/rail	$	$	$
Auto maintenance	$	$	$
Parking & tolls	$	$	$
Transportation Subtotal	$	$	$
Miscellaneous			
Subscriptions	$	$	$
Entertainment	$	$	$
Clothing	$	$	$
School supplies	$	$	$
Household maintenance	$	$	$
Personal items	$	$	$
Self-care	$	$	$
Miscellaneous Subtotal	$	$	$
Total Monthly Expenses (add all subtotal lines)	$	$	$
The Balance (subtract Total Monthly Expenses from Total Monthly Income)	$	$	$

- If the Balance is a negative number in the Budget column, you need to rethink some of your expected expenses, otherwise you'll go into debt for the month.
- If the Balance is a negative number in the Actual column, you went into debt for the month, and must now take a hard look at your spending to determine where you went too far off track. Pay closer attention to your spending in that category in the future.
- If the Balance in the Actual column is positive, you need to allocate that money somewhere—additional spending in categories important to you, particularly focusing on earmarking unspent income on paying down faster any credit-card debt, car loan, or mortgage you might have, or funneling it into additional savings. Ultimately you are trying to get to $0, meaning a balanced budget.

THE SPENDING PLAN

Many of the same processes used in a personal budget play out with a spending plan, though a spending plan provides a more detailed method of estimating, tracking, and analyzing your income and outflow on a monthly basis. Putting the plan together will take some time in the first month or two, though it shouldn't take more than about thirty minutes to an hour. After you're accustomed to how the plan works and how your money flows through the various categories each month, you'll be able to whip out and review your monthly spending plan in just a few minutes, since your income and many of your expenses generally won't change drastically from one month to the next. By the way, you might want to make several copies of the plan so that you have one available at the start of each month, or visit www.WSJ.com/BookTools and print as many copies as you need.

To use this spending plan, start with some projections. In the Projected Month Total column, estimate how much you anticipate spending in all of the categories appropriate to your life. Many won't be. Some might be missing; go ahead and pencil them in under the appropriate heading (i.e., Home, Food, Clothing, etc.). Tally all your projections near the bottom of the spending plan in the Total Expenses row.

Don't view these projections as just wild guesses you hope to meet. These ultimately form the boundaries you set for yourself in terms of both spending and saving. It does not matter if the limits you set for yourself include $500 a month at Starbucks and an equal amount downloading iTunes into your iPod. So long as you're happy with the spending decisions you make, and so long as your spending stays within the limits of your income and doesn't cut into your monthly savings, you're living within your means and there's a very good chance you'll stick to you plan.

Now, under the Income category at the bottom of the worksheet, estimate the cumulative amount of all income you expect to earn for the month. Include everything here, not just salary. Maybe you supplement your pay by painting and then selling Velvet Elvises (Elvii?) on eBay. Whatever income you expect to pocket, include it here. Keep in mind that this is after-tax income, or your take-home pay.

So you have two projected numbers now: Total Expenses and Total Income. If the latter is larger than the former, you're good to go. This means your paycheck can handle your spending for the month, and whatever extra amount of income you have remaining you can shovel into savings, an investment account, or you can return to your spending plan and assign some or all of that money to categories that are important to you that month.

If, however, your expenses are bigger, then you have a problem; you'll need to pare your expectations. Once you have your expenses equal to or smaller than your income, you're ready for the month.

You'll notice that the plan is divided into four weeks. This division helps you keep track of where you are at any point in the month in relation to your projections. In the early months, keep every receipt you receive; drop them into a jar, a basket, a drawer, or whatever container is convenient. Each week add them up for each category in which you have transactions, and jot down that number in the appropriate box for the week.

The aim of this exercise is to keep you interacting with your spending plan and to allow you to alter your plan on the fly when necessary. For instance: You've projected that for the month you'll spend no more than $200 eating out. As the final week of the month starts, you see on your spending plan that you've already spent $185 on restaurant meals, including an unexpected $90 tab you got stuck with when you and a dozen friends hit the priciest Italian eatery in town. You know instantly that you'll be noshing at home in Week Four since you only have $15 to spend on eating out and you just don't cotton to Happy Meals five nights straight.

Or, consider this: It's the second week of the month and a group of friends invites you to the beach for a long weekend. The cost: $200 for gas and food and festivities. You peek at your spending plan and see that you can cut $70 from your entertainment and can easily put off until next month that new $100 blazer you wanted. And you're more than willing to cut $30 this month from your grocery bill. Just like that, you've worked directly with your spending plan to finance a long weekend at the beach without negatively impacting your finances or relying on the good graces of American Express to front you the money.

Most traditional budgets aren't as malleable, because people often set them up once during the year and determine an average amount they expect to spend in each category. Then, they don't typically interact with their budget unless something dramatic changes, like they get a raise, buy a new car, move to a new apartment or house. Yet your spending each month is fluid because your life is fluid. As such, aside from your fixed costs, you're probably not going to routinely spend exactly that average, budgeted amount in some category. That's where budgets start to go haywire.

MONTHLY SPENDING PLAN

JANUARY

HOME	**Projected Month Total**	**Week 1**	**Week 2**	**Week 3**	**Week 4**	**Actual Month Total**	**Amount Over/Under**
Rent/Mortgage							
Property Taxes							
Home Insurance							
Telephone & Long Distance							
Cell Phone							
Oil/Gas							
Electric							
Water							
Household Supplies							
Furniture/Decorating							
Landscaping							
Services (Pest/Clean)							
Home Improvement							
Maintenance/Repair							
Total Home							
FOOD	**Projected Month Total**	**Week 1**	**Week 2**	**Week 3**	**Week 4**	**Actual Month Total**	**Amount Over/Under**
Groceries							
Dinner Out							
Lunch (weekdays)							
Lunch (weekends)							
Total Food							
CLOTHING	**Projected Month Total**	**Week 1**	**Week 2**	**Week 3**	**Week 4**	**Actual Month Total**	**Amount Over/Under**
Coats & Jackets							
Business							
Sportswear							
Lingerie							
Shoes/Purses							
Accessories							
Jewelry							
Dry Cleaning							

Alterations/Repairs							
Total Clothing							
SELF-CARE	**Projected Month Total**	**Week 1**	**Week 2**	**Week 3**	**Week 4**	**Actual Month Total**	**Amount Over/Under**
Haircut/Hair Care							
Massage/Body Work							
Health Club/Yoga							
Manicure/Pedicure							
Facial/Skin Care							
Cosmetics							
Total Self-Care							
HEALTH CARE	**Projected Month Total**	**Week 1**	**Week 2**	**Week 3**	**Week 4**	**Actual Month Total**	**Amount Over/Under**
Insurance							
Meds/Prescriptions							
Doctor							
Dentist							
Glasses/Contacts							
Therapy							
Chiro/Acupuncture							
Vitamins/Supplements							
Total Health Care							
TRANSPORTATION	**Projected Month Total**	**Week 1**	**Week 2**	**Week 3**	**Week 4**	**Actual Month Total**	**Amount Over/Under**
Car Payment							
Insurance/Registration							
Gas							
Maintenance (oil/lube)							
Repairs							
Car Wash							
Tolls							
Public Transport							
Total Transportation							

(continued)

MONTHLY SPENDING PLAN *(continued)*

ENTERTAINMENT	Projected Month Total	Week 1	Week 2	Week 3	Week 4	Actual Month Total	Amount Over/Under
Tapes/CDs							
Movies Out							
Cable/Satellite Service							
Movie Rental							
Theater/Concerts							
Sporting Events							
Magazines/Newspapers							
Books/Hobbies							
Film/Photography							
Parties/Holidays							
Babysitting Costs							
Total Entertainment							
DEPENDENT CARE	**Projected Month Total**	**Week 1**	**Week 2**	**Week 3**	**Week 4**	**Actual Month Total**	**Amount Over/Under**
Child Care							
Clothes							
Allowance							
Toys & Books							
Health Care							
Entertainment							
Sports/Camps							
Pet Food & Supplies							
Vet Bills							
Grooming							
Total Dependent Care							
VACATION/TRAVEL	**Projected Month Total**	**Week 1**	**Week 2**	**Week 3**	**Week 4**	**Actual Month Total**	**Amount Over/Under**
Airfare/Transportation							
Taxis/Buses/Rail/Toll							
Lodging							
Meals							
Excursions							
Entertainment							

Souvenirs							
Total Vacation/Travel							
GIFTS	**Projected Month Total**	**Week 1**	**Week 2**	**Week 3**	**Week 4**	**Actual Month Total**	**Amount Over/Under**
Christmas/Hanukkah							
Birthdays/Showers							
Wedding/Anniversary							
Cards							
Charitable							
Holiday Gifts (Mother's Day, etc.)							
Total Gifts							
EDUCATION	**Projected Month Total**	**Week 1**	**Week 2**	**Week 3**	**Week 4**	**Actual Month Total**	**Amount Over/Under**
Tuition							
Books/Supplies							
Fee							
School Lunch							
After-School Care							
Fundraisers							
Total Education							
PERSONAL BUSINESS	**Projected Month Total**	**Week 1**	**Week 2**	**Week 3**	**Week 4**	**Actual Month Total**	**Amount Over/Under**
Office Supplies							
Copies							
Postage							
Bank Fees							
Professional Services							
Internet Service Provider							
Total Personal Business							
INSURANCE	**Projected Month Total**	**Week 1**	**Week 2**	**Week 3**	**Week 4**	**Actual Month Total**	**Amount Over/Under**
Disability/Long-Term Care							
Life							
Total Insurance							

(continued)

MONTHLY SPENDING PLAN *(continued)*

SAVINGS/INVESTMENT	Projected Month Total	Week 1	Week 2	Week 3	Week 4	Actual Month Total	Amount Over/Under
Periodic Savings							
Monthly Savings							
Investments							
Total Savings/Investment							
DEBT REPAYMENT	Projected Month Total	Week 1	Week 2	Week 3	Week 4	Actual Month Total	Amount Over/Under
Total Debt Repayment							
MISCELLANEOUS	Projected Month Total	Week 1	Week 2	Week 3	Week 4	Actual Month Total	Amount Over/Under
Total Miscellaneous							
Total Expenses							
INCOME	Projected Month Total	Week 1	Week 2	Week 3	Week 4	Actual Month Total	Amount Over/Under
Earned Income							
Earned Income							
Earned Income							
Other Income							
Gifts							
Total Income							

MONTHLY BALANCE

		Beginning of Month	End of Month
1. Checkbook Balance	(+ or −)		
2. Cash on Hand	(+)		
3. Total Expected Income	(+)		
4. Total Money Available (1+2+3)	(=)		
5. Total Expenses	(−)		
6. Difference (4−5)	(=)		

Suppose you budget $300 on groceries every single month. Yet in four consecutive months your real costs are $270, $328, $307, and $214. You've underspent your budget by $81. But you don't really know that, so you don't know to funnel that cash elsewhere. Or maybe your monthly spending on groceries amounts to $194, $376, $297, and $355. You're over budget by $22, but you don't know enough to trim spending elsewhere. True, those differences are small, and they might be absorbed elsewhere in your budget accidentally. But two things: At some point, even small numbers add up to significant dollars; and those small numbers might not be absorbed elsewhere. It could be that you're going overbudget on all your categories—you just don't realize it. Nor do you realize you're sinking financially. More likely you just complain every month about not making enough money, or that you're struggling to make ends meet, not cognizant of the fact that you are your own worst enemy.

With a spending plan, however, you see your outlays take shape every week, giving you the power to steer them in any direction you deem necessary. In essence, you've taken control of your money, instead of feeling as though your budget has control over you.

At the bottom of the spending plan you'll find the Monthly Balance (at the top of this page). This is the built-in lie detector.

As the month begins, insert on Line 1 of the Beginning of Month column the balance in your checkbook. Add to that the cash in your wallet and your Total Expected Income for the month. This represents all the money you can spend for the month. Do not include any of the money in your savings account. Money in savings is not available—and should not be drawn upon—for everyday spending needs. Total Expenses represents your projected expenses.

The difference between Total Money Available and Total Expenses represents how much you should have remaining when the month concludes. When you're putting the plan together at the beginning of the month, Total Money Available and Total Expenses either must equal one another or the difference must be a positive number. A negative number means you will run a deficit for the month, a situation you must avoid to keep your finances healthy. If the number is negative, you must adjust your spending, or, if possible, find a way to increase your income—without tapping your savings.

When the month concludes, repeat the same process in the End of Month column: list your checkbook balance (the same as the Beginning of Month), cash on hand, and the actual amount of income you earned. List your actual expenses as recorded in the various categories on the spending plan, and subtract those expenses from the total money available to you during the month. The difference, Line 6, should match the difference at the beginning of the month. If not, you're missing either some spending or income somewhere in your life, and it's probably on the spending side.

This lie-detector is particularly useful in relationships, when partners often hide expenses from one another for whatever reason. You can instantly see if the family's spending for the month doesn't balance, and you can go back through your bank and credit-card statements and begin to piece together where the missing money went. Pay close attention to ATM withdrawals and checks made out to "Cash." Cash expenses are hard to track, whereas credit cards explicitly announce what business was paid how much money. Often, ATM transactions and checks for cash typically underlie those missing expenses since the money must come from somewhere. Debit-card transactions at places like grocery and convenience stores are another place to look. If your grocery expenses seem unusually high, the culprit could be a partner secretly snatching extra money by requesting cash back when paying for the groceries with the debit card and using the cash on personal items.

PAY YOURSELF FIRST

When you're inundated with bills each month, finding the spare cash to stuff into a savings account can seem impossible. Here's the solution: Pay yourself before you pay your bills.

LIFE IS NOT STATIC— YOUR SPENDING PLAN SHOULDN'T BE, EITHER

Though your spending changes every month to match your needs and wants, there are certain life events that necessitate that you take a much broader look at your plan and adjust it to meet changing demands on your income.

Here are a few of those major events:

- Marriage or divorce. In either situation your income changes, altering what you can afford to spend and save.
- A new job/raise/promotion or a salary decrease. An increase, among other options, allows you to budget more to a retirement savings plan; a decrease may mean you need to trim back your retirement savings to cover more immediate needs, such as housing costs.
- Birth/adoption of a child. Your spending needs to alter dramatically when kids arrive, and kids are universally more expensive than parents estimate. You will need to adjust your spending plan to make room for the added costs.
- You buy a house or car or make some large purchase. When you trade monthly rent for a mortgage, refinance your mortgage, or take on a car note, you'll need to adjust those categories on your spending plan.
- Retirement. Your income changes and so does your spending. You'll need to refigure both to ensure that your spending doesn't exceed the money you withdraw annually from your nest egg.

Your life isn't just measured in the present. You have a whole bunch of tomorrows to finance as well. Those tomorrows all arrive at a time in life when you're no longer employed but, with luck, enjoying your retirement.

We'll dig into retirement in greater depth later, but at this junction you need to consider that retirement is a bill you must pay, since the money you manage to save during your working career, along with Social Security and any pension or 401(k)-style account you might have, will be all you have to create the paycheck you'll live on when you leave work for the last time.

The first step toward saving for retirement, or toward building an emergency savings account, or toward buying a new home or car, begins with paying yourself before you pay everyone else.

That means you must work into your personal budget or your spending plan an amount of money you automatically take from your income every month and stash in a savings account, a money-market account, or a retirement account. As that money grows, you can periodically distribute it among other types of saving and investment accounts.

The rule of thumb is that you should save at least 10% of your income. Ultimately, that may or may not be enough to fund your retirement, but it's a good starting point to get you thinking about how much you currently save and what you can do to save more.

Fill in this worksheet to calculate how much you're saving currently, or visit www.WSJ.com/BookTools:

HOW MUCH ARE YOU CURRENTLY SAVING?

Annual savings in:

Savings account	________
Savings bonds	________
401(k)/403(b) plan (my contribution)	________
401(k)/403(b) plan (company contribution)	________
Traditional IRA	________
Roth IRA	________
Mutual funds	________
Brokerage accounts	________
Other	________
Total savings	$________
Annual income	$________

Savings Rate

Savings ÷ Income	________%

If you're saving 10% or more of your income, pat yourself on the back—though you should always strive to save more where you can since unexpected costs crop up in life that will mandate that you have access to cash. Rest assured that retirement is more often than not more expensive than most people plan on.

If you're saving less than 10%, there are strategies you can use to bolster your savings rate. First, sign up for your 401(k) retirement plan if you haven't already. This forces you to sock away money with every paycheck before you see the money. Start off at the minimum 1%; you'll never miss the cash. If you can afford to, start your contributions at the level equal to the company match. So, if your employer gives you 50 cents for every dollar you save, up to 4% of your salary, then try to save 4%. You're getting an immediate 50% return on your investment from the company. Some companies are even more munificent, offering a dollar-for-dollar match. That's a lot of free money you don't want to miss out on.

Every year, increase the amount you save by one percentage point; that will help you ultimately get to 10% of your salary. Also, whenever you earn a pay raise, automatically stick half the raise into your retirement plan. That way, you're saving more, and doing so painlessly, yet you still see some of the benefits of a bigger paycheck.

Another option: Save automatically outside your 401(k) plan. With mutual funds, savings accounts, savings bonds, and IRAs, you can contribute throughout the year, on a monthly or quarterly basis, to reduce that one-time shock of having to pony up a sizable sum of cash. Many employers make saving easy by automatically sending a portion of your paycheck directly to a savings account before your check makes it into your hands. Mutual-fund companies and IRA providers can arrange to automatically deduct a predetermined sum from your checking or savings account on a regular basis. Banks will automatically transfer money to a savings or money-market account from your checking account on whatever regular schedule you establish.

Suppose you decide you want to contribute $1,000 to a Roth IRA but can't seem to find a spare grand in your checking or savings. You could, instead, work $83 into your monthly spending plan and accomplish the same goal. Similarly, if your company pays you every two weeks, you could instruct your payroll department to pull money out of every paycheck and send it to the U.S. Treasury to buy a U.S. savings bond. The paper version of Series EE bonds sell for half their face value, so 26 weeks of $50 purchases is the equivalent of $2,600 worth of $100 bonds at maturity. You can find out more about savings bonds at www.savingsbonds.gov.

The point is that every paycheck earns you a new opportunity to build wealth. It may not be a get-rich-quick-scheme, but it is a get-rich-nonetheless scheme.

If nothing else, remember this: Wealth is never defined by what you earn but what you save. Learn to save and you'll learn to be wealthy. Don't think so? Consider this: Assume you can afford $200 a month on a car note for a respectable vehicle, but you decide you'd rather spend $450 to lease over a five-year period a jazzy roadster well beyond your means. And imagine your financially savvy neighbor had the same choice but opted to invest that extra $250 every month into a high-yield, online savings account that in the fall of 2005 was paying annual interest payments of 4% at several Web-based banks. At the end of five years you have nothing but an old car, probably with burger stains on the leather, and which you must return to the dealer. Your neighbor, however, has $16,575.

Who learned to be wealthy?

VALUE OF $250 INVESTED MONTHLY AT 4%

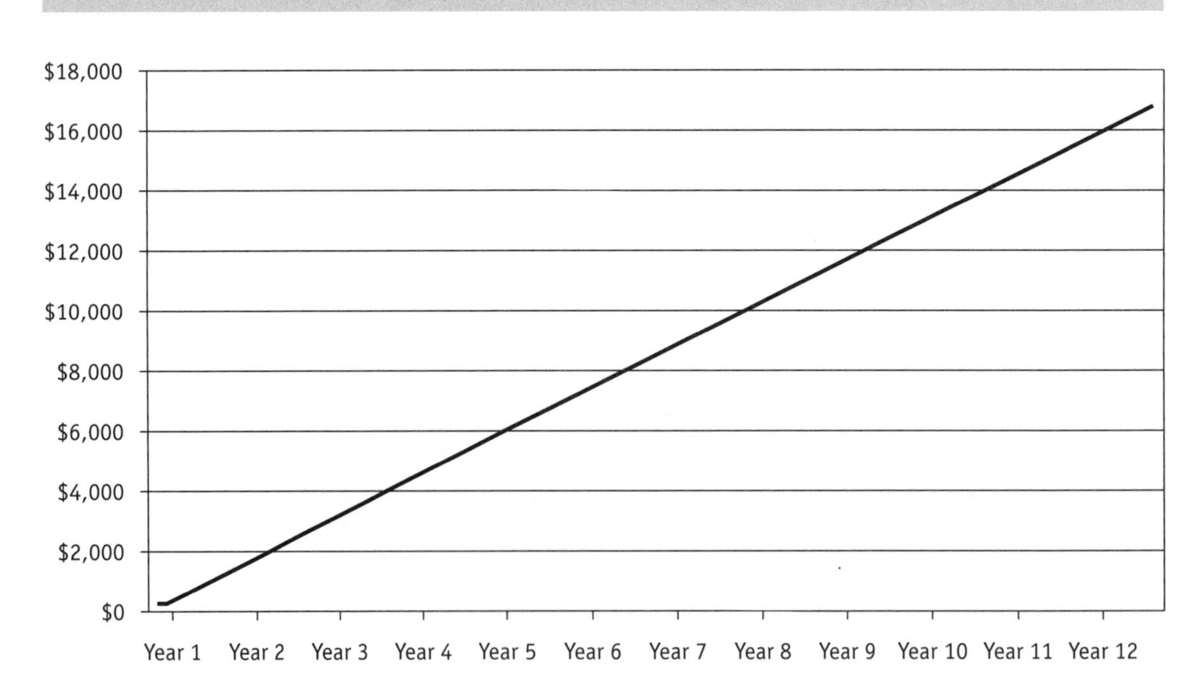

EMERGENCY SAVINGS

No budget—no personal financial life—is complete without a portion of your monthly income earmarked for an emergency savings account. This is a mandatory account for every household, because you never know when some large, unexpected expense comes along to attack your income.

When those moments arrive—and they invariably do—the ability to rely on yourself will provide a far greater degree of security, and a much-reduced level of stress, than you'd experience struggling to scrounge up the money you need by begging and borrowing from friends and family. Better to have your own financial cushion to fall back on.

What defines an emergency runs the gamut. On the small end, you might need to spring for $1,000 to cover the deductible on your auto-insurance policy if you wreck your car. Substantially more costly: losing your job and having to rely on your emergency account to cover your bills for several months. By the way, semiannual and annual insurance premiums or quarterly property-tax bills do not qualify as emergency expenses—though too often people treat them that way. Insurance premiums and property taxes are known costs that should be factored into your budget or spending plan every month, and stashed in a savings account, so that when they arise you have the money available to pay the cost without treating the bill as an unexpected surprise that you must scramble to afford.

The emergency you want to plan for is the worst you can imagine: losing your job for a period of time. At that moment, what you have accumulated in savings is the money that will tide you over until you find new employment. How much money you need in your emergency account is an individual matter, since the costs of your life will differ from your neighbor's. Your account, however, should cover the basics you need to feed, shelter, and insure your family.

The worksheet on pages 27–28 lists life's essential costs. Plug in your monthly expenses for each item and you'll have the dollar amount you spend every month on just your basic expenses.

The toughest part of building an emergency savings account is figuring out how much money to stick into it. Some financial planners say three months; some say a year. Generally speaking, the more stable your career or the greater the demand for your particular skills, the smaller your emergency savings must be to cover any time out of work you might face, since replacing your income could be relatively easy. If, however, you are the last in a long line of the typewriter-ribbon makers, and that's all you know how to make, then your emergency account needs to be much larger to cover a potentially extended period while you're out looking for a new career.

At the end of the day, only you know what the account should hold. Ask yourself: At what financial level do I feel comfortable? That will tell you how much money you need to save. Here's the formula:

Emergency Savings = Financial Comfort Level ÷ Basic Monthly Expenses

$__________ = $__________ ÷ $__________

That answer tells you how many months you could subsist on your savings before it's depleted. So, if your financial comfort level is $20,000 and your monthly expenses are $2,500, you'd have eight months of living banked away for an emergency ($20,000 ÷ $2,500 = 8). You might determine that eight months isn't enough, or is too much, allowing you to dial your comfort level up or down to meet your goal.

If you think of comfort in terms of months rather than in terms of dollars, then this is the calculation you want to use:

Emergency Savings = Basic Monthly Expenses × Number of Months Needed

$__________ = $__________ × __________

If you know you want a year's worth of expenses that amount to $3,000 a month, then you'll need to sock away $36,000 to reach your comfort zone (12 × $3,000 = $36,000).

However you determine the size of your emergency savings, once you have the number, you can begin saving to reach your goal. Simply factor into your monthly budget or spending plan an equal amount each month that puts you at your goal within whatever number of months you select. Or you can save whatever dollar amount you feel comfortable affording in a given month, knowing you'll reach your goal at some point. There's no rule that says you must reach your emergency savings target in a certain period. Remember, money is fungible and finances are flexible, and saving what you can each month while still enjoying yourself will ultimately lead to better results in the end—and in the end, success isn't measured in how you attained those result but that you, in fact, attained them at all.

EMERGENCY EXPENSES

Jot down the costs you incur each month in each category. If you don't have any costs in some particular category, skip it. Tally the totals in each category and add them all together. That number represents the monthly expenses you must pay no matter what to remain in your house with the lights on, to feed and insure your family, and to educate your children.

HOME

Rent/Mortgage ____________
Property Taxes ____________
Home Insurance ____________
Telephone & Long Distance ____________
Oil/Gas ____________
Electric ____________
Water ____________
____
Total Home $____________

FOOD

Groceries ____________
____
Total Food $____________

HEALTH CARE

Insurance ____________
Meds/Prescriptions ____________
____
Total Health Care $____________

TRANSPORTATION

Car Payment ____________
Insurance/Registration ____________
Gas ____________
Maintenance (oil/lube) ____________
____
Total Transportation $____________

(continued)

EMERGENCY EXPENSES *(continued)*

DEPENDENT CARE

Child Care ________

____

Total Dependent Care $________

EDUCATION

Tuition ________

Books/Supplies ________

Fees ________

School Lunch ________

____

Total Education $________

INSURANCE

Disability/Long-Term Care ________

Life ________

____

Total Insurance $________

DEBT REPAYMENT

____

____

Total Debt Repayment $________

MISCELLANEOUS

____

____

____

Total Miscellaneous $________

TOTAL EXPENSES $________

The caveat: You *must* save something every month, consistently. You can't slough off for a month or three to buy surfing lessons and a new board. Healthy money habits are built on the back of small, incremental, and consistent steps that relentlessly push you toward your goals with every single paycheck.

THE ANNUAL BUDGET

Inside every company, planning the spending for the new year is the equivalent of the capital budget, the list of big outlays the managers expect or want to make during the year to improve the business's operations. In a personal finance context, this is the annual budget—the big expenses you want or need to make to improve your life, whether your definition of improvement is an extra $1,200 in your savings account by year's end or a new washing machine. Building an annual budget comes after paying yourself first and establishing an emergency savings account because it's more important to establish a savings ethic and an emergency stash before you worry about budgeting for the coming year.

Don't toss your budget or spending plan into the garbage when each month ends. As each year draws to a close, gather up all your monthly plans and, using a blank spending plan or personal budget worksheet, fill in the average expense you racked up in each of the main categories, such as rent or mortgage, groceries, utilities, insurance, and such—basically the essential expenses you must pay every month. The fixed expenses will be easy to budget for the coming year since they don't change. With variable expenses like food and electricity, estimate what you expect to pay, given what you paid in the previous year. If you pay your car insurance every six months, include those semiannual costs in the appropriate month so that you don't overallocate your income in certain months.

You'll also need to estimate your monthly income. Don't forget to include any pay raises you might be eligible for, though be sure to subtract the taxes. Your human resources department can tell you exactly what your take-home pay will be, based on a new salary level.

Once you've plugged in your income and necessary expenses, you'll see how much money is left over each month. That's the money you can earmark to various causes throughout the year, the money remaining each month to spend or save as you wish on larger projects—your capital expenses.

The question becomes: What do you wish for?

On the Annual Budget worksheet list all your big, known expenses for the year that aren't on your monthly plans, as well as your big wants. Don't edit your wants; put down everything you might like to accomplish for the coming year: a new car, additional savings, a digital camera, remodelling the kitchen, a two-week vacation to New Zealand's South Island. You're not likely to get them all; in fact, you might only be able to afford one. But once you know all that you want, you can prioritize the list, then spend the year focused on attaining those items that are most important to you or which you can afford this year.

Alongside each want, pencil in the cost, either a known cost or a good estimate of what it is likely to cost. Divide each cost by 12; that's the monthly expense necessary to fund that desire. Now, this doesn't mean you have to go the entire year saving for each item before you can buy it. You can spend the money along the way, knowing that the cost has already been factored into your spending.

For instance, that trip to New Zealand, which you want to take in September. Say the all-in cost for airfare, lodging, meals, and excursions is $4,000. Second-grade math tells you that's about $333 a month. So you save that amount every month, and by August you have $2,664 squirreled away. The other $1,336 will come from your savings account, and you will replenish that withdrawal over the remainder of the year by continuing to pay $333 a month back into it. This is an amount on top of whatever else you're pumping into savings, since your goal should always be to end each year with a savings-account balance larger than the previous year. If you only withdraw and replenish, you're just treading water and that gets you nowhere.

The caveat here is this: If you have to stick the rest of a discretionary expense on a credit card because you don't have enough in savings, then that expense is probably something you should put off until your finances are strong enough to support it.

Keep your annual budget with your monthly spending plan or personal budget sheets so that you can refer to it as you prepare your finances each month. That will keep fresh in your mind your priorities and help you see how you should be spending and saving for the month to reach those goals.

The strength of an annual budget lies in the fact that it requires you to plan ahead for your wants so that you don't tax your budget—and yourself—throughout the year. If you can see beforehand what is important to you in the coming year, you can shape your month-to-month spending to meet what you

BUILDING AN ANNUAL BUDGET

At the beginning of the year, look ahead to some of the big expenses you know you will have, such as property taxes, and the expenses you'd like to make, such as a new car or vacation. Under the "Total" column, pencil in the actual amount, if you know it, or an estimation of what you're likely to spend. Then you have two choices for working this expense into your Personal Budget or your Spending Plan: (1) Divide the cost by however many months you have before the expense arrives. If you expect to take a vacation in September, then divide the cost of that trip by 8 (you want the money by August) so that you can pay for the expense by then; (2) pencil in the full cost in the month it arrives, so that you know you will have that expense during that month and you can transfer that to your budget or spending plan so that you don't forget about the cost and overspend that month. Visit www.WSJ.com/BookTools for an interactive version of this worksheet.

HOME	Total	Jan.	Feb.	March	April	May	June	July	Aug.	Sep.	Oct.	Nov.	Dec.
Property Taxes													
Furniture/Decorating													
Landscaping													
Home Improvement													
Maintenance/Repair													
Total Home													
CLOTHING													
Coats & Jackets													
Business Suits													
Jewelry													
Total Clothing													
SELF-CARE													
Health Club/Yoga													
Home Fitness Equipment													
Total Self-Care													
HEALTH CARE													
Insurance													
Dentist/Orthodontia													
Glasses/Contacts													
Total Health Care													

(continued)

TRANSPORTATION	Total	Jan.	Feb.	March	April	May	June	July	Aug.	Sep.	Oct.	Nov.	Dec.
New Car/Truck													
Insurance/Registration													
Total Transportation													
ENTERTAINMENT													
New TV/electronics													
Theater/Concert Season Pass													
Sporting Events Season Tickets													
Total Entertainment													
DEPENDENT CARE													
Sports/Camps													
Total Dependent Care													
VACATION/TRAVEL													
Airfare/Transportation													
Lodging & Meals													
Total Vacation/Travel													
GIFTS													
Christmas/Hanukkah													
Birthdays/Showers													
Wedding/Anniversary													
Charitable													
Holiday gifts (Mother's Day, etc.)													
Total Gifts													

PERSONAL BUSINESS	Total	Jan.	Feb.	March	April	May	June	July	Aug.	Sep.	Oct.	Nov.	Dec.
Office Supplies													
Total Personal Business													
INSURANCE													
Disability/Long-Term Care													
Life													
Total Insurance													
SAVINGS/INVESTMENT													
Periodic Savings													
Investments													
Total Savings/Investment													
MISCELLANEOUS													
Total Miscellaneous													
Total Expenses													

have designated a priority. Maybe that trip to New Zealand is so important that you're more than willing to cut your clothing or dining or entertainment expenses to the bone, and you cut out extraneous celebrity-style magazines and start brown-bagging it to work four days a week instead of hitting the deli every day for a $10 sandwich and soft drink.

Whatever approach you take, when you're actively involved in planning how you want to spend your money, instead of just spending as you wish and reacting to it later, your finances will improve and your savings will grow because you will naturally become a better steward of your money.

CHAPTER 2

Banking: Checking, Savings, and Certificates of Deposit

Aside from fishing wayward coins from beneath the couch cushions as a kid and shoveling them into a piggy bank, a basic checking account represents just about everyone's first real encounter with personal finance. Those first accounts are typically at the nearest branch of the same bank your parents used. Surely Mom and Dad put some thought into choosing the bank, so why not just open an account where they did?

That's probably fine when you're a teen, but as you move into your own life, your own career, and your own family, your own financial needs arise. That's when you want to put some thought into the bank you use and the type of account you bank from. And while there are numerous factors that you should weigh before settling on a particular bank and a particular account, this is the primary question you must ask yourself: **What size balance do I typically carry?**

The answer will go a long way toward determining where you bank, particularly if you maintain a small bank balance.

Because of the litany of fees that banks now charge—meeting a teller face-to-face, not using direct deposit, keeping a low balance—checking accounts can be costly. Therefore, if the average, monthly balance in your account typically falls below about $500, you'll want a basic, free checking account. Pay attention, though, to how banks define "free."

Not all banks offer truly free checking. You need to read the fine print to be clear on what you can and can't do, and what charges you'll face for various activities. To get truly free checking you need an account that:

- Requires no minimum balance
- Imposes no monthly service charge
- Levies no per-check charge

Customers who maintain a large balance need to shop around as well; banks are eager for your business and all offer a variety of services that can save you money—or make you more money. Among the perks you can find are higher interest rates, free checks, free wire transfers, free stop-payment services, and so on. And you don't necessarily need to have all your money in your checking account to benefit. Many banks let you link accounts so that the combined balance in your checking, savings, money market, and CDs counts toward your average monthly balance.

Beyond that, a variety of factors will likely play upon your banking needs. Every person has different demands, so here's a checklist of factors to reference when looking for a bank account that meets your needs. The most efficient way to shop for a bank is online, since bank Web sites routinely list all the services that come with each type of account; that will allow you to do much of your homework quickly.

CHECKING ACCOUNTS

Checking accounts are easy: You deposit money, you withdraw money, you write checks, you spend using your debit card. Easy.

And then comes the monthly headache—reconciling your checkbook register with what the bank says you have. If you could just match the number in your checkbook to the number on the statement, all would be fine. Alas, balancing a checking account doesn't typically work that way. By the time the month ends and the bank sends out your account statement, more than a week has passed, and in that time you have undoubtedly written more checks and

WHAT TYPE OF BANK SERVICES DO YOU NEED?

Shop several different banks, using this form as a guide to check off the services that are most important to you and to price the fees and account minimums. You'll need more than one copy to shop around, so print additional copies at www.WSJ.com/BookTools.

Bank: ______________ **Phone:** ______________

Location: ______________

CHECKING ACCOUNT

- ☐ Minimum balance required (minimum: $ ______)
- ☐ Monthly fee (fee: $ ______)
- ☐ Per-check charge ($ ______)
- ☐ Interest paid (rate: ______ %)
- ☐ Overdraft protection through linked account
- ☐ Online bill-pay services
- ☐ Branch close to home (Location: ______________)
- ☐ Internet services, including online transfers
- ☐ Wire transfers
- ☐ Foreign currency availability
- ☐ Direct deposit
- ☐ Wide ATM network
- ☐ Linked accounts to waive fees
- ☐ Branch close to work (Location: ______________)

SAVINGS ACCOUNT

- ☐ Minimum balance required (minimum: $ ______)
- ☐ Minimum amount to open account (minimum: $ ______)
- ☐ Fee for not maintaining minimum (fee: $ ______)
- ☐ Unlimited monthly transactions (# of transactions: ______)
- ☐ Link to checking to provide overdraft protection
- ☐ Annual percentage yield (______ %)

MONEY MARKET ACCOUNT

- ☐ Annual percentage yield (______ %)
- ☐ Minimum balance required (minimum: $ ______)
- ☐ Check-writing privileges
- ☐ Minimum amount to open account (minimum: $ ______)
- ☐ Link to checking to provide overdraft protection
- ☐ Monthly fee (fee: $ ______)
- ☐ Maximum monthly transactions (# of transactions: ______)
- ☐ Excess transaction fee ($ ______)
- ☐ Fee to access account through phone or teller
- ☐ Fee for not maintaining minimum (fee: $ ______)

CERTIFICATE OF DEPOSIT (CD)

- ☐ Annual interest rate (______ %)
- ☐ Maturity date (date: ______)
- ☐ Ability to increase rate during CD term
- ☐ Term (months: ______)
- ☐ Penalty for early withdrawal (penalty: ______)
- ☐ Minimum amount to open account (minimum: $ ______)

BALANCING A CHECKBOOK

Step 1: Mark off in your checkbook all the deposits and credits that are accounted for in this month's statement. Be sure to mark off the matching entries on the statement as well.

Step 2: Add to you checkbook register all the deposits, credits, and interest payments you received during the month that are not already included in your checkbook. Mark these items off in the register and on the statement.

Step 3: Subtract from your checkbook all the service charges, automated monthly deductions, unrecorded checks, and ATM or debit transactions that you forgot to record when they happened. Again, mark these items off in the register and on the statement.

Step 4: In the column to the immediate right on the following page, list all checks in your register that are not listed in your current statement. These are checks you've written but as of this statement remain unpaid by your bank.

Step 5: In the column to the far right, list all the deposits in your register that are not listed in your current statement. These are deposits you've made, and while the money is available in your account, the sum hasn't flowed through your statement yet.

Step 6: Enter the Ending Balance on your statement: ____________________

Step 7: Enter the total amount of deposits from the column at the far right: + ____________________

Step 8: Subtotal (add Step 7 to Step 6): ____________________

Step 9: Enter the total amount of the unpaid checks from the column at the immediate right: – ____________________

Step 10: Subtract Step 9 from Step 8. This number should match the number in your checkbook register: ____________________

List Unpaid Checks	
Check #	**Amount**
Total $	

List Deposits	
Date	**Deposit Amount**
Total $	

If your statement doesn't match your checkbook register, here are some hints to help you:

- Go back and add up all the unpaid checks and deposits in the two columns above to make sure you didn't miscalculate or punch a stray digit into your calculator.
- Go back and redo the math in your checkbook register to make sure your addition and subtraction through the month was accurate.
- Compare the entries in your checkbook against the entries on the statement to make sure that you didn't accidentally record in your checkbook a check for $19.21 that was actually only $19.12 according to your statement.
- Be sure you added the interest payment to your register or subtracted service fees you were charged.
- If your checkbook still refuses to match your statement, you may need to "force balance" your account. See the next worksheet (page 41).

withdrawn more money and used your debit card at the grocery store and your ATM card on the way to work and you've deposited your paycheck—and the net effect of it is that your checkbook register looks nothing like your bank-statement balance.

A lot of people never balance their checkbooks. They just keep a running tab on the last line in their checkbook register and hope or assume it's vaguely accurate. That's a pretty cavalier way to manage your money. You risk being overdrawn and having to shell out fees needlessly, or you risk not knowing you have more money than you suspect—funds that might reduce the financial stress you're feeling come the end of every month; funds you might use to invest in an individual retirement account you didn't think you could afford; funds you might use to buy that new TV and replace the one that picks up thirteen channels of snow and a community-access station broadcasting nothing but local zoning-board meetings.

Balancing your checkbook is an easy task, though at times certainly frustrating when, after an hour of calculating and refiguring, your checkbook and bank statement are still Zip codes apart. No fret, here's how to make the numbers work: Break out the calculator or a pencil and paper and follow the simple ten-step worksheet on pages 38–39.

If after using the worksheet you still can't get your checkbook register to match your monthly statement, you can do one of two things: (1) go to your local bank branch and tell one of the bankers sitting at a desk (not a teller at the counter) that you're having problems reconciling your account and could you please have a copy of your account history going back three months. You'll have to compare it, line for line, to your register, but it will show you items that you may have overlooked over the months. You could also ask the banker to help you if you're really stumped. (2) You can "force balance" your account, essentially accepting the balance the bank shows.

These same worksheets can be used to balance your savings accounts as well.

CERTIFICATES OF DEPOSIT—AND WHEN BREAKING ONE MAKES SENSE

In large measure, certificates of deposit—simply called CDs—are an investment and could just as well be part of the second half of this workbook, where you'll find the tools and strategies for investing in stocks and bonds and mutual funds.

FORCE BALANCING A CHECKBOOK

Step 1: Enter the Ending Balance on this month's statement: ____________

Step 2: Look back on the Balancing a Checkbook worksheet and enter the total amount for the unpaid checks: – ____________

Step 3: Subtract Step 2 from Step 1: ____________

Step 4: Look back on the Balancing a Checkbook worksheet and enter the total amount of the deposits that didn't appear on this month's statement: + ____________

Step 5: Add Step 4 to Step 3. This is your forced balance. Enter this number in your checkbook as your current balance: ____________

Yet, just as checking accounts are typically the first personal finance account for many people, CDs are frequently one of the first nonchecking bank accounts people pursue—and one of the last, too, since retirees routinely rely on the income they generate from CDs. The reason is because CDs are easy to understand and entirely safe in that they're backed by the Federal Deposit Insurance Corporation, the FDIC, meaning that even if your bank fails, the money and interest you've accumulated in your CD will be returned to you in full—so long as the amount is less than $100,000.

In short, CDs are more souped-up savings accounts than what most people consider to be an investment. That goes, too, for CD ladders, which we'll get into shortly. Moreover, they're a very good place to begin building your financial base before stepping up to the world of investing and Wall Street.

CDs are simple to understand: You deposit your money and promise not to withdraw it for anywhere from one month to ten years. Because of that promise the bank offers you a premium interest rate, higher than you would typically earn on a standard savings account. The bank does this because it knows it can invest your money for a set amount of time and earn some income for itself.

In general, when interest rates are heading up, you want to stick to short-term CDs, nothing longer than about a year. This will allow you relatively quick access to your money, giving you the opportunity to roll your cash into higher-yielding CDs as interest rates escalate.

WHEN IT MAKES SENSE TO BREAK A CERTIFICATE OF DEPOSIT

If you're considering a short-term certificate of deposit because you don't want to lock your money up beyond a certain number of years, consider whether you might actually earn more by investing in a longer-term CD that you cash out of—or break—when the shorter term CD would have matured. Visit www.WSJ.com/BookTools for an interactive version of this worksheet:

		Example		Worksheet	
		CD #1	CD #2	CD #1	CD #2
Line 1	Principal amount of CD	$10,000	$10,000		
Line 2	Interest rate	4.50%	3.50%		
Line 3	Original Term in months	60	24		
Line 4	Term in Years for CD #2	2			
Line 5	Money Factor (find on Future Value chart, pages 43–44, where the rate on Line 2 intersects with the term in years on Line 4)	1.094	1.0724		
Line 6	Value of CDs at end of CD #2 Term (Line 1 × Line 5)	$10,940	$10,724		

Penalty

Now, calculate the interest earned in the last three months—or four, five, or six months; whatever penalty your bank charges. Start by determining the value of the CD prior to the penalty. Remember, there is no penalty on CD #2.

		Example	Worksheet
Line 7	Enter the number of months worth of interest you lose for breaking the CD:	3	
Line 8	Multiple Line 4 times 12, then subtract Line 7 ((2 × 12) − 3)	21	
Line 9	Term in Years of Line 8 (21 ÷ 12)	1¾	
Line 10	Money Factor (locate on Future Value chart, pages 43–44, where rate on Line 2 intersects Term in Years on Line 9)	1.0818	
Line 11	Multiply Line 1 by Line 10. This is the CD's value after the penalty	$10,818	
Line 12	Subtract the value of CD #2 on Line 6 from Line 11. If positive, the longer-term CD wins out. If this is negative, stick with the short-term CD	$94	

THE FUTURE VALUE OF $1, COMPOUNDED MONTHLY

YEAR	RATE 1.0%	1.25%	1.5%	1.75%	2.0%	2.25%	2.5%	2.75%	3.0%	3.25%	3.5%	3.75%	4.0%	4.25%	4.5%	4.75%	5.0%	5.25%	5.5%
1/4	1.0025	1.0031	1.0038	1.0044	1.0050	1.0056	1.0063	1.0069	1.0075	1.0081	1.0088	1.0094	1.0100	1.0107	1.0113	1.0119	1.0126	1.0132	1.0138
1/2	1.0050	1.0063	1.0075	1.0088	1.0100	1.0113	1.0126	1.0138	1.0151	1.0164	1.0176	1.0189	1.0202	1.0214	1.0227	1.0240	1.0253	1.0265	1.0278
3/4	1.0075	1.0094	1.0113	1.0132	1.0151	1.0170	1.0189	1.0208	1.0227	1.0246	1.0266	1.0285	1.0304	1.0323	1.0343	1.0362	1.0381	1.0401	1.0420
1	1.0100	1.0126	1.0151	1.0176	1.0202	1.0227	1.0253	1.0278	1.0304	1.0330	1.0356	1.0382	1.0407	1.0433	1.0459	1.0485	1.0512	1.0538	1.0564
1 1/4	1.0126	1.0157	1.0189	1.0221	1.0253	1.0285	1.0317	1.0349	1.0382	1.0414	1.0447	1.0479	1.0512	1.0545	1.0578	1.0610	1.0644	1.0677	1.0710
1 1/2	1.0151	1.0189	1.0227	1.0266	1.0304	1.0343	1.0382	1.0421	1.0460	1.0499	1.0538	1.0578	1.0617	1.0657	1.0697	1.0737	1.0777	1.0817	1.0858
1 3/4	1.0176	1.0221	1.0266	1.0311	1.0356	1.0401	1.0447	1.0492	1.0538	1.0584	1.0631	1.0677	1.0724	1.0771	1.0818	1.0865	1.0912	1.0960	1.1008
2	1.0202	1.0253	1.0304	1.0356	1.0408	1.0460	1.0512	1.0565	1.0618	1.0671	1.0724	1.0778	1.0831	1.0886	1.0940	1.0995	1.1049	1.1105	1.1160
2 1/4	1.0227	1.0285	1.0343	1.0401	1.0460	1.0519	1.0578	1.0638	1.0697	1.0758	1.0818	1.0879	1.0940	1.1002	1.1063	1.1126	1.1188	1.1251	1.1314
2 1/2	1.0253	1.0317	1.0382	1.0447	1.0512	1.0578	1.0644	1.0711	1.0778	1.0845	1.0913	1.0981	1.1050	1.1119	1.1188	1.1258	1.1329	1.1399	1.1470
2 3/4	1.0279	1.0350	1.0421	1.0493	1.0565	1.0638	1.0711	1.0785	1.0859	1.0934	1.1009	1.1085	1.1161	1.1237	1.1315	1.1392	1.1471	1.1550	1.1629
3	1.0304	1.0382	1.0460	1.0539	1.0618	1.0698	1.0778	1.0859	1.0941	1.1023	1.1105	1.1189	1.1273	1.1357	1.1442	1.1528	1.1615	1.1702	1.1789
3 1/4	1.0330	1.0414	1.0499	1.0585	1.0671	1.0758	1.0846	1.0934	1.1023	1.1112	1.1203	1.1294	1.1386	1.1478	1.1572	1.1666	1.1761	1.1856	1.1952
3 1/2	1.0356	1.0447	1.0539	1.0631	1.0724	1.0819	1.0913	1.1009	1.1106	1.1203	1.1301	1.1400	1.1500	1.1601	1.1702	1.1805	1.1908	1.2012	1.2117
3 3/4	1.0382	1.0480	1.0578	1.0678	1.0778	1.0880	1.0982	1.1085	1.1189	1.1294	1.1400	1.1507	1.1615	1.1724	1.1835	1.1946	1.2058	1.2171	1.2285
4	1.0408	1.0512	1.0618	1.0725	1.0832	1.0941	1.1051	1.1161	1.1273	1.1386	1.1500	1.1616	1.1732	1.1849	1.1968	1.2088	1.2209	1.2331	1.2455
4 1/4	1.0434	1.0545	1.0658	1.0772	1.0886	1.1002	1.1120	1.1238	1.1358	1.1479	1.1601	1.1725	1.1850	1.1976	1.2103	1.2232	1.2362	1.2494	1.2627
4 1/2	1.0460	1.0578	1.0698	1.0819	1.0941	1.1064	1.1189	1.1316	1.1443	1.1573	1.1703	1.1835	1.1969	1.2104	1.2240	1.2378	1.2517	1.2658	1.2801
4 3/4	1.0486	1.0611	1.0738	1.0866	1.0996	1.1127	1.1259	1.1394	1.1529	1.1667	1.1806	1.1946	1.2089	1.2233	1.2378	1.2525	1.2674	1.2825	1.2978
5	1.0512	1.0645	1.0778	1.0914	1.1051	1.1190	1.1330	1.1472	1.1616	1.1762	1.1909	1.2059	1.2210	1.2363	1.2518	1.2675	1.2834	1.2994	1.3157
5 1/4	1.0539	1.0678	1.0819	1.0962	1.1106	1.1253	1.1401	1.1551	1.1704	1.1858	1.2014	1.2172	1.2332	1.2495	1.2659	1.2826	1.2995	1.3166	1.3339
5 1/2	1.0565	1.0711	1.0859	1.1010	1.1162	1.1316	1.1472	1.1631	1.1792	1.1954	1.2119	1.2287	1.2456	1.2628	1.2802	1.2979	1.3158	1.3339	1.3523
5 3/4	1.0592	1.0745	1.0900	1.1058	1.1218	1.1380	1.1544	1.1711	1.1880	1.2052	1.2226	1.2402	1.2581	1.2763	1.2947	1.3134	1.3323	1.3515	1.3710
6	1.0618	1.0778	1.0941	1.1106	1.1274	1.1444	1.1617	1.1792	1.1969	1.2150	1.2333	1.2519	1.2707	1.2899	1.3093	1.3290	1.3490	1.3693	1.3899
6 1/4	1.0645	1.0812	1.0982	1.1155	1.1330	1.1508	1.1689	1.1873	1.2059	1.2249	1.2441	1.2637	1.2835	1.3036	1.3241	1.3449	1.3660	1.3874	1.4091
6 1/2	1.0671	1.0846	1.1023	1.1204	1.1387	1.1573	1.1762	1.1955	1.2150	1.2349	1.2550	1.2755	1.2964	1.3175	1.3390	1.3609	1.3831	1.4057	1.4286
6 3/4	1.0698	1.0880	1.1065	1.1253	1.1444	1.1638	1.1836	1.2037	1.2242	1.2449	1.2661	1.2875	1.3094	1.3316	1.3542	1.3771	1.4005	1.4242	1.4483
7	1.0725	1.0914	1.1106	1.1302	1.1501	1.1704	1.1910	1.2120	1.2334	1.2551	1.2772	1.2996	1.3225	1.3458	1.3695	1.3935	1.4180	1.4430	1.4683
7 1/4	1.0752	1.0948	1.1148	1.1352	1.1559	1.1770	1.1985	1.2204	1.2426	1.2653	1.2884	1.3119	1.3358	1.3601	1.3849	1.4101	1.4358	1.4620	1.4886
7 1/2	1.0779	1.0982	1.1190	1.1401	1.1617	1.1836	1.2060	1.2288	1.2520	1.2756	1.2997	1.3242	1.3492	1.3746	1.4006	1.4270	1.4539	1.4813	1.5092
7 3/4	1.0805	1.1017	1.1232	1.1451	1.1675	1.1903	1.2135	1.2372	1.2614	1.2860	1.3111	1.3367	1.3627	1.3893	1.4164	1.4440	1.4721	1.5008	1.5300
8	1.0833	1.1051	1.1274	1.1502	1.1734	1.1970	1.2211	1.2458	1.2709	1.2965	1.3226	1.3492	1.3764	1.4041	1.4324	1.4612	1.4906	1.5206	1.5511
8 1/4	1.0860	1.1086	1.1316	1.1552	1.1792	1.2038	1.2288	1.2543	1.2804	1.3070	1.3342	1.3619	1.3902	1.4191	1.4485	1.4786	1.5093	1.5406	1.5726
8 1/2	1.0887	1.1120	1.1359	1.1603	1.1851	1.2105	1.2365	1.2630	1.2901	1.3177	1.3459	1.3747	1.4042	1.4342	1.4649	1.4962	1.5282	1.5609	1.5943
8 3/4	1.0914	1.1155	1.1402	1.1653	1.1911	1.2174	1.2442	1.2717	1.2998	1.3284	1.3577	1.3877	1.4182	1.4495	1.4814	1.5141	1.5474	1.5815	1.6163
9	1.0941	1.1190	1.1444	1.1704	1.1970	1.2242	1.2520	1.2805	1.3095	1.3392	1.3696	1.4007	1.4325	1.4650	1.4982	1.5321	1.5668	1.6023	1.6386
9 1/4	1.0969	1.1225	1.1487	1.1756	1.2030	1.2311	1.2599	1.2893	1.3194	1.3502	1.3817	1.4139	1.4468	1.4806	1.5151	1.5504	1.5865	1.6235	1.6613
9 1/2	1.0996	1.1260	1.1531	1.1807	1.2091	1.2381	1.2678	1.2982	1.3293	1.3612	1.3938	1.4272	1.4614	1.4964	1.5322	1.5689	1.6064	1.6449	1.6842
9 3/4	1.1024	1.1295	1.1574	1.1859	1.2151	1.2450	1.2757	1.3071	1.3393	1.3722	1.4060	1.4406	1.4760	1.5123	1.5495	1.5876	1.6266	1.6666	1.7075
10	1.1051	1.1331	1.1617	1.1911	1.2212	1.2521	1.2837	1.3161	1.3494	1.3834	1.4183	1.4541	1.4908	1.5284	1.5670	1.6065	1.6470	1.6885	1.7311

(continued)

THE FUTURE VALUE OF $1, COMPOUNDED MONTHLY *(continued)*

	RATE																	
YEAR	5.75%	6.0%	6.25%	6.5%	6.75%	7.0%	7.25%	7.5%	7.75%	8.0%	8.25%	8.5%	8.75%	9.0%	9.25%	9.5%	9.75%	10.0%
¼	1.0144	1.0151	1.0157	1.0163	1.0170	1.0176	1.0182	1.0189	1.0195	1.0201	1.0208	1.0214	1.0220	1.0227	1.0233	1.0239	1.0246	1.0252
½	1.0291	1.0304	1.0317	1.0329	1.0342	1.0355	1.0368	1.0381	1.0394	1.0407	1.0420	1.0433	1.0446	1.0459	1.0472	1.0485	1.0498	1.0511
¾	1.0440	1.0459	1.0479	1.0498	1.0518	1.0537	1.0557	1.0577	1.0596	1.0616	1.0636	1.0656	1.0676	1.0696	1.0716	1.0735	1.0755	1.0775
1	1.0590	1.0617	1.0643	1.0670	1.0696	1.0723	1.0750	1.0776	1.0803	1.0830	1.0857	1.0884	1.0911	1.0938	1.0965	1.0992	1.1020	1.1047
1¼	1.0743	1.0777	1.0810	1.0844	1.0878	1.0912	1.0946	1.0980	1.1014	1.1048	1.1082	1.1117	1.1151	1.1186	1.1221	1.1256	1.1291	1.1326
1½	1.0899	1.0939	1.0980	1.1021	1.1062	1.1104	1.1145	1.1187	1.1229	1.1270	1.1313	1.1355	1.1397	1.1440	1.1482	1.1525	1.1568	1.1611
1¾	1.1056	1.1104	1.1153	1.1201	1.1250	1.1299	1.1348	1.1398	1.1448	1.1497	1.1547	1.1598	1.1648	1.1699	1.1750	1.1801	1.1852	1.1904
2	1.1216	1.1272	1.1328	1.1384	1.1441	1.1498	1.1555	1.1613	1.1671	1.1729	1.1787	1.1846	1.1905	1.1964	1.2024	1.2083	1.2144	1.2204
2¼	1.1378	1.1442	1.1506	1.1570	1.1635	1.1700	1.1766	1.1832	1.1898	1.1965	1.2032	1.2099	1.2167	1.2235	1.2304	1.2373	1.2442	1.2512
2½	1.1542	1.1614	1.1686	1.1759	1.1833	1.1906	1.1981	1.2055	1.2130	1.2206	1.2282	1.2358	1.2435	1.2513	1.2591	1.2669	1.2748	1.2827
2¾	1.1709	1.1789	1.1870	1.1951	1.2033	1.2116	1.2199	1.2283	1.2367	1.2452	1.2537	1.2623	1.2709	1.2796	1.2884	1.2972	1.3061	1.3150
3	1.1878	1.1967	1.2056	1.2147	1.2238	1.2329	1.2422	1.2514	1.2608	1.2702	1.2797	1.2893	1.2989	1.3086	1.3184	1.3283	1.3382	1.3482
3¼	1.2049	1.2147	1.2246	1.2345	1.2445	1.2546	1.2648	1.2751	1.2854	1.2958	1.3063	1.3169	1.3276	1.3383	1.3491	1.3601	1.3711	1.3822
3½	1.2223	1.2330	1.2438	1.2547	1.2657	1.2767	1.2879	1.2991	1.3105	1.3219	1.3334	1.3451	1.3568	1.3686	1.3806	1.3926	1.4048	1.4170
3¾	1.2400	1.2516	1.2633	1.2752	1.2871	1.2992	1.3113	1.3236	1.3360	1.3485	1.3611	1.3739	1.3867	1.3997	1.4128	1.4260	1.4393	1.4527
4	1.2579	1.2705	1.2832	1.2960	1.3090	1.3221	1.3353	1.3486	1.3621	1.3757	1.3894	1.4033	1.4173	1.4314	1.4457	1.4601	1.4747	1.4894
4¼	1.2761	1.2896	1.3033	1.3172	1.3312	1.3453	1.3596	1.3740	1.3886	1.4034	1.4183	1.4333	1.4485	1.4639	1.4794	1.4951	1.5109	1.5269
4½	1.2945	1.3091	1.3238	1.3387	1.3538	1.3690	1.3844	1.4000	1.4157	1.4316	1.4477	1.4640	1.4804	1.4970	1.5138	1.5308	1.5480	1.5654
4¾	1.3132	1.3288	1.3446	1.3606	1.3768	1.3931	1.4096	1.4264	1.4433	1.4604	1.4778	1.4953	1.5130	1.5310	1.5491	1.5675	1.5861	1.6049
5	1.3322	1.3489	1.3657	1.3828	1.4001	1.4176	1.4354	1.4533	1.4715	1.4898	1.5085	1.5273	1.5464	1.5657	1.5852	1.6050	1.6250	1.6453
5¼	1.3514	1.3692	1.3872	1.4054	1.4239	1.4426	1.4615	1.4807	1.5002	1.5198	1.5398	1.5600	1.5804	1.6012	1.6222	1.6434	1.6650	1.6868
5½	1.3709	1.3898	1.4090	1.4284	1.4480	1.4680	1.4882	1.5087	1.5294	1.5504	1.5718	1.5934	1.6153	1.6375	1.6600	1.6828	1.7059	1.7293
5¾	1.3907	1.4108	1.4311	1.4517	1.4726	1.4938	1.5153	1.5371	1.5592	1.5817	1.6044	1.6275	1.6509	1.6746	1.6987	1.7231	1.7478	1.7729
6	1.4108	1.4320	1.4536	1.4754	1.4976	1.5201	1.5429	1.5661	1.5896	1.6135	1.6377	1.6623	1.6872	1.7126	1.7382	1.7643	1.7908	1.8176
6¼	1.4312	1.4536	1.4764	1.4995	1.5230	1.5469	1.5711	1.5957	1.6206	1.6460	1.6717	1.6979	1.7244	1.7514	1.7787	1.8065	1.8348	1.8634
6½	1.4519	1.4755	1.4996	1.5240	1.5489	1.5741	1.5997	1.6258	1.6522	1.6791	1.7064	1.7342	1.7624	1.7911	1.8202	1.8498	1.8798	1.9104
6¾	1.4728	1.4978	1.5231	1.5489	1.5751	1.6018	1.6289	1.6564	1.6845	1.7129	1.7419	1.7713	1.8013	1.8317	1.8626	1.8941	1.9260	1.9585
7	1.4941	1.5204	1.5471	1.5742	1.6019	1.6300	1.6586	1.6877	1.7173	1.7474	1.7781	1.8092	1.8409	1.8732	1.9060	1.9394	1.9734	2.0079
7¼	1.5157	1.5433	1.5714	1.6000	1.6291	1.6587	1.6888	1.7195	1.7508	1.7826	1.8150	1.8480	1.8815	1.9157	1.9504	1.9858	2.0219	2.0585
7½	1.5376	1.5666	1.5961	1.6261	1.6567	1.6879	1.7196	1.7520	1.7849	1.8185	1.8527	1.8875	1.9230	1.9591	1.9959	2.0334	2.0715	2.1104
7¾	1.5598	1.5902	1.6211	1.6527	1.6848	1.7176	1.7510	1.7850	1.8197	1.8551	1.8912	1.9279	1.9653	2.0035	2.0424	2.0820	2.1225	2.1636
8	1.5823	1.6141	1.6466	1.6797	1.7134	1.7478	1.7829	1.8187	1.8552	1.8925	1.9304	1.9692	2.0086	2.0489	2.0900	2.1319	2.1746	2.2182
8¼	1.6052	1.6385	1.6724	1.7071	1.7425	1.7786	1.8154	1.8530	1.8914	1.9306	1.9705	2.0113	2.0529	2.0954	2.1387	2.1829	2.2280	2.2741
8½	1.6284	1.6632	1.6987	1.7350	1.7721	1.8099	1.8485	1.8880	1.9283	1.9694	2.0114	2.0543	2.0981	2.1429	2.1885	2.2352	2.2828	2.3314
8¾	1.6519	1.6882	1.7254	1.7633	1.8021	1.8418	1.8822	1.9236	1.9659	2.0091	2.0532	2.0983	2.1444	2.1914	2.2395	2.2887	2.3389	2.3902
9	1.6758	1.7137	1.7525	1.7922	1.8327	1.8742	1.9166	1.9599	2.0042	2.0495	2.0959	2.1432	2.1916	2.2411	2.2917	2.3435	2.3964	2.4504
9¼	1.7000	1.7395	1.7800	1.8214	1.8638	1.9072	1.9515	1.9969	2.0433	2.0908	2.1394	2.1891	2.2399	2.2919	2.3451	2.3996	2.4553	2.5122
9½	1.7245	1.7658	1.8080	1.8512	1.8954	1.9407	1.9871	2.0346	2.0832	2.1329	2.1838	2.2359	2.2893	2.3439	2.3998	2.4570	2.5156	2.5756
9¾	1.7494	1.7924	1.8364	1.8814	1.9276	1.9749	2.0233	2.0730	2.1238	2.1758	2.2292	2.2838	2.3397	2.3970	2.4557	2.5158	2.5774	2.6405
10	1.7747	1.8194	1.8652	1.9122	1.9603	2.0097	2.0602	2.1121	2.1652	2.2196	2.2754	2.3326	2.3913	2.4514	2.5129	2.5761	2.6407	2.7070

When rates are headed south, however, you want to lock into longer-term CDs, since you'll be locking in an interest rate that is likely far superior to what your peers will earn months or years later when rates are down. During an inflationary bout in the late 1970s and early '80s, savers who purchased CDs with durations of ten years and longer were looking mighty flush by the early 1990s, when rates had fallen to mid-single digits or below.

Banks typically impose an early withdrawal penalty if you reclaim your money before a CD matures. Withdrawing your money early is known as breaking a CD, and you'll typically pay a penalty equal to three months' worth of interest. Generally, you don't want to break a CD because of the income loss you face. For that reason, you shouldn't invest in a long-term CD if you might need the money early.

However, in the category of every-rule-has-its-exception, there are times when it makes sense financially to stick your cash in the longer-term certificate, knowing full well that you intend to break the CD at some point. One time to do this: when long-term CD rates are high enough and the penalty low enough that the net interest payments you receive still outstrip what you would have earned in a shorter-term CD.

Your banker certainly isn't going to tell you about this because if you invest in a five-year CD, well, the bank fully expects to have use of your money for all five years; the bank doesn't want you coming back early to get your money, since that means the bank loses the opportunity to earn income by investing your deposit elsewhere. Consider a situation in which a five-year CD offers a rate of 4.5%, while a two-year CD pays 3.5%. At the end of two years a $10,000 two-year CD would return $10,724. Over that same two-year period the five-year CD would return $10,940, though you do have to account for the penalty you'll pay to break the certificate—in this case three months' worth, or a bit more than $122. That still leaves you with nearly $10,818, about $94 more than you'd have with the shorter-term CD.

For savvy consumers, investing in longer-term CDs with the intention of breaking them early can make sense. Just pay attention to the size of the penalty, since the money that will be subtracted from your account when you reclaim the cash early plays a leading role in this sort of transaction.

WHAT INFLATION REALLY MEANS

While the dollars you have in your pocket today look identical to the dollars in your pocket last year, those dollars last year were worth more. Through the years, inflation—defined as the tendency of prices to rise over time—erodes the value of your money.

What does that mean? In short, it means the goods you buy today require that you spend more dollars than you had to spend last year for the same items.

In a very simple example, a loaf of bread that cost $1.50 in January 2004 would cost $1.54 a year later. Four cents doesn't sound like much to fret about, but when you spread that increase—2.67%—across your entire span of purchases in a given year, and then you spread inflation over years and decades, you're talking about differences of many dollars. For instance, that same $1.50 purchase in 1955 would cost $10.31 in 2005.

This chart shows the real effects of inflation on $1 in the 50 years between 1955 and 2005. Notice the dramatic leaps in the 1970s and 1980s, when inflation in the U.S. hit double-digit levels.

50 YEARS OF INFLATION

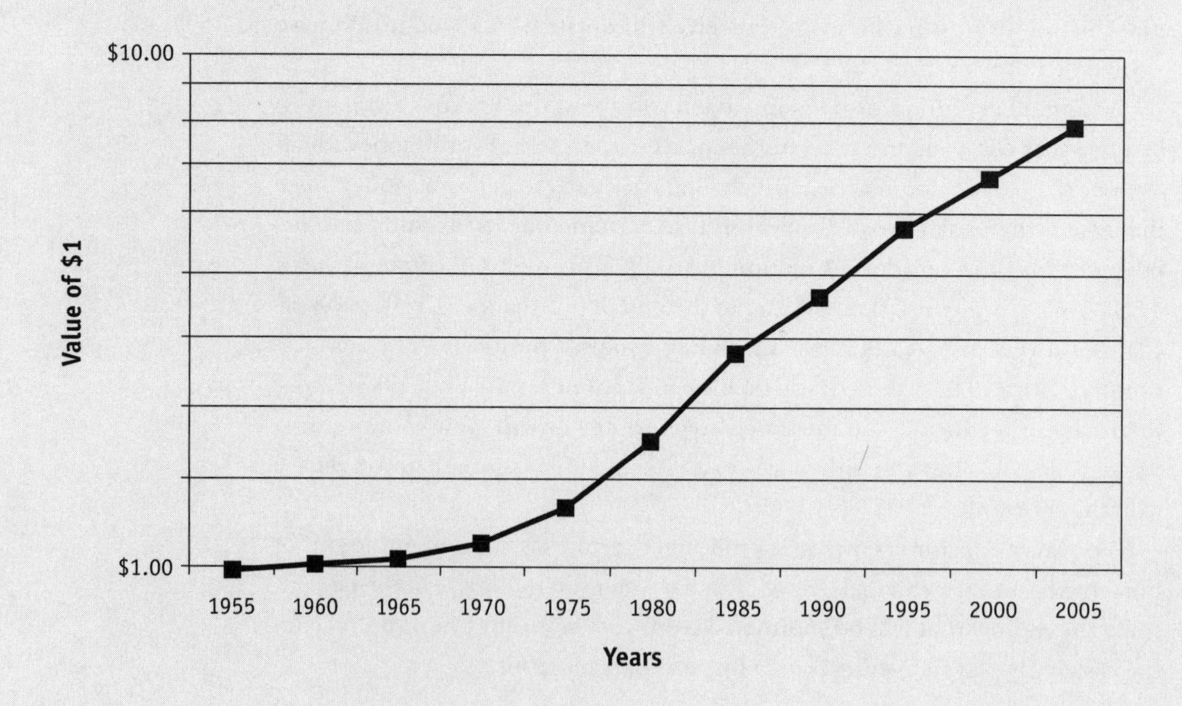

BUILDING A CD LADDER

Laddering is a simple concept: Spread your available cash—"ladder" it—across a variety of time periods as a means of interest-rate diversification. With a CD ladder a portion of your cash remains liquid, yet you ultimately earn more money.

Why a ladder, of all metaphors? Well, the individual CDs symbolize rungs on a figurative ladder, each one a little farther away, and the higher you climb, the higher the rate.

It works like this: Say you have $10,000 you want to put into a CD. Short-term rates don't excite you, yet the higher rates mean you must lock away all your money for longer than you want. So, split the difference. Put one-fifth (or some such fraction) in a one-year CD, another fifth in a two-year CD, and keep building a ladder until you put the last $2,000 in a five-year CD. As each CD matures, roll it over into another five-year contract; that will keep each rung on your ladder filled out, since at the end of Year 1 your two-year CD is now a one-year CD and your three-year is now a two-year and so on.

This strategy offers two benefits: (1) You have the opportunity to tap your short-term money when it comes due, if you need it, rather than having all your cash locked up for the long haul; and (2) a big chunk of dollars works harder for you over the longer term, rather than earning paltry returns if you had invested all of your money in a short-term account. So, you get the best of both worlds: higher returns and greater liquidity.

A $10,000 CD ladder might look something like this:

	CD #1	CD #2	CD #3	CD #4	CD #5
CD Value	$2,000	$2,000	$2,000	$2,000	$2,000
Rate	3%	3.25%	3.75%	4%	4.5%
Time Period	1 year	2 years	3 years	4 years	5 years
Return	$2,061	$2,134	$2,238	$2,346	$2,504

Remember this rule-of-thumb with CDs: When interest rates are falling, you want to put as much money as you feel comfortable locking up into long-term CDs; that way you'll earn the highest rates for the longest period of time. When interest rates are rising, you want most of your dollars in short-term CDs; that way you roll out of lower-paying CDs quickly and into ones with higher rates.

CHAPTER 3

Planning: Preparing for the Worst

Or, When Bad Things Happen to Good Finances

The Boy Scout motto—always be prepared—should be stamped atop every financial document.

Preparation is one of the cornerstones of financial success and financial security, since you never know what trouble might visit. If you're unprepared, whatever event arises can seriously undermine—or destroy—your or your family's finances.

Preparing for the worst means preparing for the bad moments, big and small. It means knowing what you own in the event that a disaster demolishes it; it means keeping track of what's in your wallet in case it comes up lost or stolen. It means storing the right documents in the right places so that those that are necessary in an emergency aren't locked away from you or those who need access. And, in the worst situation, it means preparing for the possibility of a premature death that impacts the family's income.

INSURANCE

No one necessarily likes to buy insurance. At best, the purchase seems such a waste: You're paying all this money every year and not really seeing any benefit from it, if you're lucky. Think about it: How often do you wreck your car? How often is your house damaged or your possessions stolen? Those events are so rare in most lives that if state laws and mortgage-company demands didn't dictate insurance coverage on your car and house, a lot of folks would just skip the expense of insurance all together.

Yet insurance is rooted in sound finance and is just as important as a savings account, only from a reverse perspective: it won't necessarily make you any money, but it can keep you from losing the money you do have—and that's just as significant. After all, think of how challenging it would be to replace a car (yours or someone else's you destroyed), or to rebuild a home, or to restock all of your damaged or stolen possessions. Each of these can be exceedingly expensive and reach so deep into your savings that you don't begin to have enough to cover the loss.

When you stop to think about it, insurance is one of the smartest financial products you can own, since it protects you and your family from potentially catastrophic losses that you could never pay for on your own. For that reason, insurance, despite the feeling that the premiums represent money wasted, is instead money well spent—so long as you're not overpaying for the coverage or overinsuring your needs.

One of the most important forms of insurance coverage for a family is life insurance, since the unexpected death of a breadwinner can visit serious financial hardships upon a family, leaving a surviving spouse unable to pay for the necessities of life.

DO I NEED INSURANCE?

Many people skip life insurance because they don't think they need it. In truth, not everyone does.

If no one depends upon you financially, you probably don't need the coverage. But if you have dependents—for instance, children, a nonworking spouse, parents you support, a special-needs family member—life insurance is necessary so that you can still provide for their needs if something unfortunate happens to you. This chart will help you determine whether you need coverage and explain why you do and don't, depending upon your situation:

WHO NEEDS INSURANCE?

Who You Are	Insurance Needs?	Rationale
Single	No	In the vast majority of cases you have no dependents who would be financially impacted by your death. The caveat: If you do have a dependent of some sort—be it a child, special-needs sibling, etc.—then you do need coverage.
Single Parent	Yes	By definition, you have a dependent who would suffer without a source of financial support if you die. Life insurance is mandatory for you.
Married: dual income, no kids	No	If you or your spouse can fend for yourself in the event either of you died unexpectedly, you generally don't need life insurance, since neither is financially dependent upon the other. The caveat: Funeral and burial costs can be very expensive, so a small policy that covers those costs can relieve some of the immediate financial pressure of an untimely death.
Married: dual income, with kids	Yes	Even though both spouses are employed, the death of one leaves the other as a single parent still facing the same financial obligations you both would have managed together. Life insurance is necessary to help cover the living expenses of the dependents, as well as education costs.
Married: one income, kids or no kids	Yes	In either situation, you have dependents—whether it's the nonworking spouse or the spouse and the kids. This situation also raises the question of whether to insure a nonworking spouse. The answer: Yes. In such a case the working spouse isn't looking to replace lost income, but is looking for the income to replace lost services the nonworking spouse provided, particularly child-care needs.
Retired	No	If you're retired and your kids are grown and living on their own, and you have amassed some assets to help see you through retirement, you generally don't need life insurance, since you have no income to replace. The caveat: You want to leave a large estate to your heirs; a life insurance policy can cover whatever estate taxes might be due. Or, if you still have several years to pay on a mortgage, you might want a policy that would help a surviving spouse manage that obligation.

HOW MUCH INSURANCE DO I NEED?

The answer to this question depends on what type of coverage you're talking about: life, auto, or home.

Auto Coverage

Your state generally mandates a minimum that you must carry. But those minimums can leave you feeling maximum pain if you ever cause a wreck that totals another car or results in bodily injury or death to another person. You're likely to be sued for more than the minimums your insurance provides.

Thus, to the degree you can afford it, the appropriate amount of auto coverage is enough to protect the amount of assets you have accumulated, since those assets are at risk in a car wreck. Remember that your car represents your biggest liability because cars all too frequently destroy other cars and kill, maim, or injure people. That generates big-dollar lawsuits—the very reason you want as much insurance protection as you can afford.

If that much insurance is too pricey—even with a higher deductible that lowers the premium—then at least go as high as your finances will allow.

In general, "minimum" coverage is whatever your particular state deems the lowest amount of liability insurance you must carry. "Regular" coverage typically pays liabilities up to $50,000 per person and $100,000 per accident. "Premium" coverage goes up to $100,000 per person and $300,000 per accident. And "ultra" coverage is $300,000/$300,000 or, with some insurers, $250,000/$500,000. Various insurers use different designations for the various types of coverage—such as ultra and premium—but the liability limits are generally similar.

Home Owner's Coverage

People often insure their home for the purchase price, though that's not necessarily the right amount. Your home typically includes land, and no matter whether your house is destroyed by fire, wind, or flood, the land isn't going anywhere. As such, there's no reason to insure the purchase price, since that price includes the value of the land. And in high-rent districts like the metropolitan East Coast or coastal California, the land value can far outstrip the value of the home.

What you want to insure is the cost of rebuilding the home. And what is that cost? Well, ask a local builder how much you'd have to pay to build a replica of your house, inside and out. If you have a high-end gourmet kitchen, triple-crown molding throughout, and wide-plank pinewood floors, make sure those finishing details are factored in. Don't rely on the recent sales price of a nearby home; again, that price includes the value of the land.

Whatever the final tally, that's how much you want to insure your home for. But just to be safe, be sure to buy a policy that provides for "replacement cost" coverage. With this coverage, an insurer will cover the stated value of the policy, plus an additional amount, usually 20% to 25%. So, if you determine your home would cost, say, $325,000 to rebuild, a $325,000 policy would actually cover as much as $406,250 in costs.

One other point about home owner's insurance: Inventory your home. Yes, this is a monstrous chore since homes are packed with so much "stuff." Yet if ever a disaster arrives, if ever your home is flooded or burned in a fire, you'll want to provide an insurance adjuster a complete accounting of what you had inside. This will help expedite a process with as little stress on you as possible. After all, with so many other challenges in your life at that moment, you're not going to want to struggle with trying to come up with a list of what you owned. Instead, use the worksheet on the next page to catalog your possessions. Videotape the inside of your home, as well, as additional proof of your possessions. The tape will also show what the finish work in your home looked like, which can come in handy as well. Keep this document and the video in a safe-deposit box away from your home. If your home is demolished in a disaster or a fire, the document and tape will likely be lost or damaged beyond use.

NOTE: A lender might tell you that you must carry insurance to cover the amount of the mortgage (which includes the land value), but that's not necessarily true. Many states impose laws that prevent lenders from requiring you carry coverage greater than that needed to rebuild your home. Resist such a push and you can save potentially hundreds of dollars a year on your home owner's policy.

Life Insurance

This coverage comes in two basic forms: cash-value and term-life. The former acts as a life-insurance policy and savings account rolled into one investment; the latter is pure life insurance.

Because a portion of your cash-value premium goes into a savings component, the amount of insurance coverage you buy is less than you'd get with a

PERSONAL PROPERTY CHECKLIST

Businesses keep inventories of all their assets. So should you. If an unfortunate disaster visits your home, knowing exactly what you own, what you paid for it and when, and any model or serial number will allow you to immediately get to work with your insurer replacing the contents of your home or apartment. Keep any receipts you have and any you get in the future.

	Item	Model/Serial Number	Date of Purchase	Purchase Price	Receipt?
LIVING/FAMILY ROOM					
DINING ROOM					
KITCHEN					

	Item	Model/Serial Number	Date of Purchase	Purchase Price	Receipt?
UTILITY ROOM					
BEDROOM 1					
BEDROOM 2					
BEDROOM 3					
HOME OFFICE/STUDY					

(continued)

	Item	Model/Serial Number	Date of Purchase	Purchase Price	Receipt?
OTHER ROOM					
CHINA/SILVERWARE					
COLLECTIBLES					
ART/JEWELRY/ANTIQUES					

term-life policy charging the exact same premium. For that reason, term-life tends to be the best option for affording as cheaply as possible as much insurance as possible. Additionally, the fees and expenses inside an insurance policy typically make them a poor choice for saving. Better to buy as much term-life as you need, and put whatever would have otherwise gone into the cash-value savings component into a low-cost mutual fund tracking the Standard & Poor's 500-stock index.

But how much insurance do you need? Figuring out the answer can feel like guessing at the number of BBs in a ten-gallon jar—wild speculation.

You have several ways to calculate a number. The simplest approach is to use the rule-of-thumb that says you should buy an amount of insurance equal to between five and ten times your annual take-home pay. (The reason to use take-home pay instead of your annual salary is that insurance payouts are not taxed, thus there's no need to replace pre-tax income.) Many people use seven as an adequate middle ground. To wit: if you bring home $50,000 a year (after taxes), you'd buy a policy that pays out $350,000.

Life Insurance Needs = Annual Take-Home Pay × 7

_______________ = _________________ × 7

That rule-of-thumb is better than nothing, since it at least provides some level of protection for your family. But it's not a very accurate indicator of your needs, unless you have no other obligations in life except to help your spouse pay monthly bills in the event of your untimely death.

Most people, however, have many other expenses they'd want to cover in their lives, and, thus, want to leave behind enough money to cover after their death—be it a mortgage they want to pay off, a college education they want to afford for their kids, or helping a surviving spouse cover retirement needs. That requires a more detailed calculation, since you need to determine just what those costs are in order to buy an appropriate amount of insurance.

The worksheet on page 58 is useful no matter whether you go with a cash-value or term-life policy, since ultimately you're purchasing a policy to cover a specific dollar amount of insurance in the event you or your spouse dies prematurely.

What makes insurance one of life's biggest chores is shopping for it. With every phone call to every agency you must run through the same long litany of

HOW MUCH LIFE INSURANCE DO I NEED?

The most challenging entry on this worksheet is the family-expense fund. This is the amount of money the surviving spouse and any children will need to live on through the years. Here's how to estimate it (visit www.WSJ.com/BookTools for an interactive version of this worksheet):

FAMILY-EXPENSE FUND

1. Your monthly income $__________
2. Multiply Line 1 by the percent of income you wish to cover. 75% to 80% is a good estimate. This covers necessities: food, utilities, clothing, transportation. Include the mortgage payment here if a surviving spouse will pay it over time; or exclude it if your life insurance will pay off the remaining balance. __________
3. Surviving spouse's take-home pay, if any, and Social Security survivor's benefits. __________
4. Subtract Item 3 from Item 2. This is the monthly shortfall the surviving spouse and family would have. __________
5. Multiply Item 4 by 12 to annualize the amount. __________
6. Multiply Item 5 by the number of years the surviving spouse and family will need the replacement income. Since that can be tough to gauge, the safe assumption is to insure the income for as many years as it takes your currently youngest child to reach college graduation. This is your **Family-Expense Fund** to insert below. [ ]

FUTURE FAMILY NEEDS

Family-expense fund	$__________
Child care	__________
Emergency fund	__________
Mortgage payoff	__________
Debt payoff	__________
College costs	__________
Retirement fund	__________
Other special needs	__________
Total Needs	[ ]

CURRENT ASSETS

Cash/Savings			$
Home equity			
Investments			
	Stocks		
	Bonds		
	Mutual funds		
	Other		
		Subtotal	
Retirement plans			
	IRAs		
	401(k)		
	Pension		
	Other		
		Subtotal	
Current life insurance			
Other assets			
		Total Assets	

INSURANCE NEEDS

Total Needs	
Total Assets	–
Insurance Needs	

personal data, vehicle identification numbers, information on your house, and on and on. Still, just like with buying a car or a house, you never accept the first quote you get from an insurance company because chances are very good you'll find a better deal if you shop around a little.

This worksheet will help you keep track of who you've called and the details of the quotes and coverage so that you can make fair comparisons between insurers.

SHOPPING FOR INSURANCE

You can use this worksheet no matter if you're shopping for home, auto, or life insurance, or an umbrella policy. You'll probably need a few more of these worksheets to shop around, and you can have many as you need at www.WSJ.com/BookTools.

Insurance company: ____________________ Phone: ____________

Contact person: ____________________

Type of coverage: (circle) Auto Home Life

Coverage amounts: [ ] Length of term: ________

Premium payment schedule: (circle) Monthly Quarterly Semiannual Annual

Total Annualized Premium: [ ]

Insurance company: ____________________ Phone: ____________

Contact person: ____________________

Type of coverage: (circle) Auto Home Life

Coverage amounts: [ ] Length of term: ________

Premium payment schedule: (circle) Monthly Quarterly Semiannual Annual

Total Annualized Premium: [ ]

Insurance company: ____________________ Phone: ____________

Contact person: ____________________

Type of coverage: (circle) Auto Home Life

Coverage amounts: [ ] Length of term: ________

Premium payment schedule: (circle) Monthly Quarterly Semiannual Annual

Total Annualized Premium: [ ]

CHAPTER 4

Borrowing: Accumulating and Managing Debt

Unless you're independently wealthy and can afford cash for your cars and homes and whatever else you want to buy, you will inevitably approach a lender at some point to borrow money to complete a purchase. The amount borrowed might be substantial, such as hundreds of thousands of dollars for a house; or it might be small—$10 on your credit card for a Chinese take-out meal for two.

Whatever the case and whatever the cost, the underlying rules are the same: someone, or some institution, is fronting you the money for a purchase, and in return you're obligating yourself to repay that money with interest.

But debt is not the same as cash, though many people treat it that way. They see a $10,000 credit limit on their Visa card and, to them, they have $10,000 to spend. Borrowing doesn't work that way. What you spend isn't money that's just gone, as it would be if you pulled the cash out of a checking or savings account. What you spend still exists, as a debit balance next to your name and is therefore money that you must, by law, replace. You might have a $10,000 credit limit, but if you have no way to repay that $10,000 you spent, then your life is in for a wooly ride as you struggle to meet minimum payments mandated by a lender or, worse, slip into bankruptcy and, if you're in a marriage, place strains on your relationship.

So let's start at the end, with signs that you may already have gone overboard with your borrowing.

WARNING SIGNS YOU CARRY TOO MUCH DEBT

- You're stressed out every month about your ability to pay down your debt.
- You have more than one credit card and you can only afford minimum payments on each.
- You pay off other bills by taking cash advances against your credit card(s).
- You have maxed out the credit line on one or more credit cards.
- You're unsure of how much combined debt you actually have.
- You live from paycheck to paycheck and can't afford to save.
- You have no savings account to fall back on in an emergency, or a savings account so small that one or two bills in the first month would wipe it out.
- You lease a car that you could not have afforded to buy using conventional bank financing.
- You rely on an interest-only mortgage to afford a house for which you otherwise could not afford the monthly payments using a conventional mortgage.
- You shop compulsively.
- You and your spouse fight about spending or the amount of the charges on a credit-card statement.
- You lie to your spouse about how you spend money, or you either hide or throw away the portion of the credit-card statement that details the expenses.
- You've been denied credit.

If any of those ring true in your life, you likely have a debt problem, and you should seek help in getting a handle on your spending so that you can begin to eradicate the debt you owe. If you can't control your debt or your spending, deeply embedded emotional issues may be at play and you should seek out a financial counselor or a financial planner who has experience dealing with emotions related to money, since many financial problems stem from emotional roots rather than monetary. You can find the Association for Financial Counseling and Planning Education at www.afcpe.org, or track down a local financial planner through the Financial Planning Association (www.fpanet.org) or the National Association of Personal Financial Advisors (www.napfa.org). Ask planners that you speak with if they or anyone on their staff deals with the emotional issues of saving and spending, or if they can refer you to someone who does.

IS YOUR DEBT TOO HIGH?

Lenders and credit counselors look at something called your "debt-to-income ratio" to gauge whether you're carrying too much debt relative to the size of your paycheck. This is, in essence, the barometer of your fiscal health.

A reading below 15%—that is, your total nonmortgage debt as a percentage of your income—is considered healthy. Less than 10% is ideal. Above 15% and you're skating toward trouble. Once you exceed 20%, lenders generally consider that you're carrying too much debt. You might be able to manage that debt load, but lenders would be concerned that any financial hiccup could send you reeling. At levels above about 35% you represent a significant risk—to yourself and to a lender.

Calculating your debt-to-income ratio is fairly straightforward. In this worksheet, do not include your mortgage (or rent), since that is not consumer debt. Instead, include all your credit-card, auto-loan or -lease, and home-equity loans and lines of credit, and any other loans you have outstanding (visit www.WSJ.com/BookTools for an interactive version of this worksheet):

CALCULATING YOUR DEBT-TO-INCOME RATIO

Credit Provider	Monthly Payment
Total Monthly Debt	

Debt-to-Income Calculation

Total monthly debt ÷ Monthly after-tax income = Debt-to-income ratio

$________ ÷ $________ = ________%

What Your Reading Means

10% or below	You're managing your credit well.
10% to 20%	You're still a good credit risk.
20% to 30%	You're bordering on being a bad credit risk.
30% and above	You're a high risk, and might need credit counseling.

PAYING DOWN DEBT

There are six degrees of separation between you and a zero balance on your consumer-credit accounts:

1. Determine How Much You Owe

Too many consumers don't really know how much debt they have. Their wallets are packed with a couple—or several—credit cards, probably a gas card or two, and a few store-branded cards for certain retailers they frequent. And the thing is, a couple hundred dollars accumulated on an individual credit card seems manageable in the abstract because the human mind is expert at compartmentalizing. You don't think about owing $10,000 in the aggregate; you only think of the $600 on a particular Visa you have in your wallet and, well, that little bit of money doesn't seem like all that much.

That aggregate, however, is key. If you can quantify the problem—and you can by simply adding together all your debt—you immediately establish the finish line you're running toward, the total amount of debt you must pay off. Though the distance involved can seem insurmountable, it's not.

TOTAL DEBT OWED

List all the credit cards you own, home-equity loans and lines-of-credit you have outstanding, auto loans/leases and any other consumer debt you owe. Exclude your mortgage. The total monthly payment will help you put into perspective the degree to which your debt is consuming your income. The phone number, meanwhile, will serve as future reference when you need to call and close your account or negotiate a lower rate with a creditor.

Creditor	Current Balance	Minimum Monthly Payment	Phone Number
Total			

2. Pay Attention to Your Spending and What You Tell Yourself

Never fall prey to the thought of "Oh well, what's another $50?" When you're struggling under thousands of dollars of debt and it's dinnertime and you're thinking "I can go to Taco Cheapo or that new sushi joint," too often people in that situation choose the expensive meal because (a) it's a seemingly affordable luxury in their life; and (b) they think that because they already owe MasterCard $10,000, well, what's another $50?

Another $50 is another $50 you could pay toward your credit-card balance to reduce your debt faster. It doesn't seem like much, but then again the first $50 you rang up on the march to $10,000 wasn't much either. Over time, seemingly inconsequential ripples lead to a wave of change.

3. Always Pay More than the Minimum Due on Your Credit Cards Each Month

And to the extent you can, add a little something extra to your car loan or any home-equity loan you have. Paying more than the minimum provides three benefits: you pay down your balance sooner, and you reduce the amount of interest you ultimately must pay, which lets you keep more of your money for other purposes.

To accomplish this, factor debt reduction into your personal budget or spending plan each month. Instead of allocating all of your disposable income to entertainment or clothes or books or whatever, earmark at least 10% or more of that money for debt repayment. If you want to be Draconian, use all of your disposable income—that which doesn't go to mandatory expenses—to repay your debt quicker.

However, don't feel like a financial failure if you have to pay down your debt at a slower pace than you would like. So long as you remain committed to shrinking that balance to zero, and so long as you see progress in that direction each month, you have reason to feel good about your efforts.

4. Holster Your Credit Cards and Rely on Cash

If you don't have the money on you at the exact moment you want to buy something, even if it's just a $1.30 diet soda at the drive-through that would first require a trip to the ATM for cash, don't buy it. Little expenses seem like nothing; after all, you can't buy a new house or a dream vacation or a retirement nest egg $1.30 at a time.

Still, small expenses accumulate during the day and over the course of a month, and if you're tossing off $1.30 here and $3.60 there, soon enough you're talking about hundreds of dollars and, over the course of a year, thousands of dollars.

That's particularly true with much larger expenses, the kind you didn't expect to make but which you nonetheless pursue, and for which you whip out the credit card to pay. You probably know the situation well: You're walking through Wal-Mart, there to buy a $3 bottle of dish detergent, and you spy a DVD you've been dying to see—you know the DVD player is on the fritz, but there's one on sale for $89, which seems pretty darn affordable—so you walk out of Wal-Mart with that $3 bottle of dish detergent and a DVD player and a DVD that cost you about $100 combined.

The best solution: Keep your credit cards away from your wallet. You'll hear in many places that you should cut up your credit cards and only use cash or a debit card. But that's illogical advice in an electronic age, when you need credit cards to efficiently shop online or to reserve a car or hotel. A better bet is to simply keep your credit cards at home, in a safe place, locked away. That way you can't just rip one out of the wallet to buy whatever has captured your fancy at the moment.

Better still, when your credit card is at home, you must drive home to fetch it. That drive home and then back to the store provides time to cool your jets and think about whether you really want—or need—to spend this money on an item that earlier in the day you weren't even thinking about.

5. Pay Off the Smallest Balance First

This doesn't necessarily jibe with conventional wisdom that says you should first pay off the card with the highest interest rate. Yet by concentrating on extinguishing the smallest balance first, you see more quickly the fruits of your labor. That will keep you motivated.

Just keep moving up the line of cards, picking the one with the next-lowest balance. This approach is ultimately more expensive, since the cards with the biggest balances are attacked last. But there's a way around that: Apply for a low-rate credit card designed for consumers who want to transfer over the balance from higher-rate cards. You can find these "balance transfer" cards at www.creditcards.com. Alternatively, call the credit-card company that's charging you the highest rate and negotiate that rate down. So many credit-card providers are competing for business that you may have some luck in persuading yours to lower your interest rate, lest you bolt for a competitor. Be nice, remind the agent that you've been a good customer for years and that you carry a balance, but that you're thinking of transferring the balance to a new card with a lower rate if the company can't reduce the rate it's charging you.

6. Cancel Cards or Close Accounts When You Pay Off the Balance

If you have several credit cards or other types of credit-based accounts, closing them down when your balance reaches zero—and cutting up the cards—will keep you from ever racking up another dime in debt on that card.

The caveat: Do not close a credit card account that you have owned for years. Your credit score is calculated, in part, on how long you've had credit in your name. If you close the oldest account, then the second oldest account reestablishes your credit history, and depending on the spread of years between those accounts you could actually be hurting your credit score. If your oldest account happens to be the one that also sports the highest interest rate, no worries; just don't use the card. Keep it active, maybe by using it once every few months to buy gas or groceries and pay it off in full. But use a low-rate card if you're going to carry a balance.

BUYING A HOME

Owning a home is the core of the American dream. It's also a very expensive proposition, given that the median price of a home in the U.S. in 2005 was nearing $200,000.

The vast majority of Americans don't have that kind of spare cash lying around. Yet roughly 70% of the population owned a home as of 2005. For that, Americans have a mortgage to thank.

Though it's thought of as a loan, a mortgage is actually not a loan, but a lien. Moreover, a mortgage is not something a lender gives you but rather something you give a lender—namely a legal security (the mortgage, itself) that gives the lender the right to take possession of the property should you default on repaying the money you borrowed to buy that particular piece of property in the first place.

But maybe you aren't convinced you want to own a home to begin with. After all, houses are a pricey proposition, given that there's more involved than just paying the monthly note. Before you buy a house, you must ask yourself if doing so really makes sense to your current financial situation and your lifestyle. You don't really want to face the prospect of buying a house, then deciding a few months later that you'd rather live in another city. You'll rack up thousands of dollars in loses from the fees and commissions you pay to buy and sell.

RENTING VERSUS BUYING: WEIGHING THE TRADE-OFFS

The benefits of home ownership are manifest: First, you build equity in an asset, meaning that with each monthly mortgage payment you own an increasingly bigger piece of the property. Second, home values tend to rise over time, usually alongside the rate of inflation—though in some cities and during certain periods of time home prices can rise much faster. That means the value of your property grows larger through the years, creating a store of value you can tap one day later in life. Third, the federal government helps you afford your home by allowing you to write off a portion of the monthly cost in the form of a deduction for the mortgage interest you pay.

Of course, some downsides exist, too. You're responsible for all manner of upkeep through the years and that eats into your ability to save or afford other expenses. Your freedom to move on a whim across town or across the country is limited since you have a home you must first sell. There's no promise that home prices will rise; they could fall, and you could lose money.

In essence, the question of covering your head with a roof comes down to this: Do you want to build equity in a piece of property, or do you want the freedom not to worry about repairing a busted toilet and mowing the lawn? That's the first step in determining whether you are ultimately a renter or a buyer, and the worksheet on page 71 can help you determine the annual cost of buying versus renting (visit www.WSJ.com/BookTools for an interactive version of this worksheet):

You might be a renter if	You might be a home owner if
you don't expect to live in one place very long, or if you want the freedom to pack up and split in an instant, renting can't be beat.	you expect to set roots in your community and want the feeling of permanency in your life.
you have no interest in unclogging toilets, fixing leaky roofs, terminating the termites, or manicuring the lawn—and no interest in paying for any of that.	you like unclogging toilets and tinkering on things around the house, or you enjoy gardening and lawn work (or at the very least don't mind paying for it).
the thought of carrying tens, and more likely hundreds of thousands, of dollars in debt makes you nauseous.	the thought of dumping thousands of dollars a year into a landlord's pocket instead of increasing your own net worth makes you nauseous.
you enjoy the amenities of apartment living, such as swimming pools and playgrounds for the kids and a workout room or handball court that you otherwise couldn't afford to purchase separately or build into your house.	you want the tax break Uncle Sam offers on the mortgage interest you pay each year, as well as the opportunity to accumulate as much as $250,000 in profits ($500,000 as a couple) tax-free when you sell.
you don't mind that your rent will increase over time.	you love the fact that your housing payment will never change, assuming you have a fixed-rate mortgage.

In the worksheet example on the next page, the cost of buying a house is about $300 cheaper every year. That's not to imply buying is always cheaper. Sometimes renting is cheaper. But remember this: The cost of monthly rent escalates alongside inflation, while the cost of a monthly mortgage payment tied to a fixed-rate loan never changes. So even in situations where renting is cheaper at first, it could become substantially more costly over time in comparison to a

WHETHER A BUYER OR A RENTER BE

ANNUAL RENTAL COSTS	Example	Your Costs
Monthly rent ($1300 × 12)	$15,600	
Utilities ($200 × 12)	$ 2,400	
Annual renter's insurance	$ 300	
Total Annual Rental Costs	**$18,300**	

ANNUAL HOUSING COSTS		Example		Your Costs
Total mortgage payments ($1,137.72 × 12)*		$13,653		
Private mortgage insurance (× 12)		$ 0		
Annual property taxes		$ 4,000		
Annual home owner's insurance		$ 1,200		
Maintenance/repairs ($150 × 12)		$ 1,800		
Utilities ($300 × 12)		$ 3,600		
Total Annual Housing Costs		**$24,253**		
Tax savings from mortgage interest deduction:				
Interest paid on mortgage:†	$11,641			
Annual property taxes:	$ 4,000			
	$15,641			
× income-tax rate‡	0.27			
Tax savings	$ 4,223	($4,223)		
Annual equity accumulated		($2,012)		
(Interest paid on mortgage − Total mortgage payments)				
Net Annual Cost of Buying		**$18,018**		
Annual Difference Between Renting and Buying		**− $282**		

*Assumes a 6.5%, 30-year fixed-rate mortgage on a $225,000 home, with a 20% down payment. If you put down less than 20%, you might have to pay PMI, or private mortgage insurance. If so, you'll need to include that cost as well.

†Interest paid on mortgage and annual equity accumulated comes from an amortization table that shows how your monthly payments are split between principal and interest. Your lender can provide an amortization table, or you can calculate one online, based on your specific mortgage, at www.hsh.com.

‡Income tax rate is the marginal rate at which your income is taxed. 27% is assumed.

mortgage payment. After all, an apartment originally costing $750 a month will cost roughly $1,000 a month after 10 years of 3% inflation, while a fixed-rate mortgage that cost $900 a month will still cost $900 a month a decade later.

HOW MUCH CAN YOU AFFORD?

Knowing whether you can afford the $12 petite filet or the $20 porterhouse at the local meatery is pretty simple. Knowing you can't afford a $70,000 Mercedes on a $20,000 income is pretty simple. But when it comes to how much house you can afford, suddenly it's not so simple.

When you start talking hundreds of thousands of dollars spread over thirty years, determining what is and is not in your financial neighborhood grows much more complex. When you add in the various interest-rate possibilities, well that only muddies the matter more.

Not to worry: The house you can afford is not the one you think is affordable; it's the one the lender says you can afford—because that's the one for which the lender will loan you the necessary funds. You don't have to visit a lender, however, to figure out how much money you can borrow and, thus, how much house you can afford.

All lenders use a formula of one sort of another to determine how much money they'll lend you. Those formulas flow directly from the size of your salary and the amount of debt you already carry. Everything else being equal, if you and your coworker have identical incomes, but you have a mound of debt, your coworker will be able to afford more house than you because a lender isn't going to offer you as much money, since your salary must repay not just the mortgage but your other debt obligations as well.

Lenders generally use two formulas—a front-end ratio and a back-end ratio. So, let's calculate them as the lenders would.

- The **front-end ratio** is the portion of your income that you can allocate to mortgage debt. This number varies by lender, but it tends to gravitate in the 28%-to-31% range. This means that no more than 31% of your gross monthly income—your income before taxes—can go to a mortgage payment.

  The math looks like this:

Front-End Ratio = Monthly Salary × 28%

___________ = ___________ × 0.28

So if you earn $50,000 a year, or $4,167 a month, a lender generally will only provide a loan amount that keeps your monthly payments under $1,167 a month.

- The back-end ratio is the portion of your income that you can allocate to all debt, including mortgage, credit-card, child-support, and any other loan payments. Lenders use back-end ratios ranging from about 36% up through 50%, though they generally congregate around 40%.

  The math:

Back-End Ratio = Monthly Salary × 36%
__________ = __________ × 0.36

With that same $50,000 income, a lender will want your total debt payments to be no more than about $1,500 a month.

Lenders will typically choose the lower number of the two calculations, but not always. So it's wise for you to know what those two numbers are and what number a lender will use. You want to determine for yourself whether you're comfortable paying whatever amount the formulas show you can afford to pay. Moreover, with either of those numbers you can calculate exactly how much house you can buy. That will keep you focused on realistic homes instead of wasting your efforts touring those beyond your wallet's ability to pay.

The worksheet on the following page will help you calculate all those ratios and determine the price range in which you should be hunting. You can also visit www.WSJ.com/BookTools for an interactive version of this worksheet.

Remember: When you're determining what size house you can afford, the mortgage isn't the only number you need to know. You'll also have to pay property taxes and insurance. Taken together this is known as the PITI, or **p**rincipal, **i**nterest, **t**axes, and **i**nsurance.

The simple formula:

Monthly House Note = Mortgage Payment (principal & interest) + Taxes + Insurance

In most instances, your lender will package your mortgage payment, taxes, and insurance into one monthly note. The lender strips out the taxes and insurance and stashes that money in an escrow account in your name, and each year pays your home owner's insurance and property taxes for you with that money.

HOW MUCH HOUSE CAN YOU AFFORD?

FRONT-END RATIO		Example		Your House
Gross monthly income		$5,000		
Many lenders limit your housing expense to 28% of your gross monthly income. But change this to reflect what your lender allows.		× 0.28		×
Front-end maximum mortgage		**$1,400**		

BACK-END RATIO		Example		Your House
Gross monthly income		$5,000		
Lenders generally limit your total debt payments to 36% of your gross monthly income. But change this to reflect what your lender allows.		× 0.36		×
Preliminary monthly mortgage		**$1,800**		
Debt obligations				
Car loan	$265			
Credit-card(s) minimum	$80			
Child support				
Student loans				
Other				
Total Monthly Debt Payments		$345		
Back-end maximum mortgage				
(subtract total monthly debt from preliminary monthly mortgage)		**$1,455**		
Record the smaller of the Front-End or Back-End maximum mortgage		$1,400		
Subtract estimated monthly taxes (or call tax assessor)		– ($150)		–
Subtract estimated monthly insurance payment (or call agent for quote)		– ($100)		–
Monthly payment on which to base purchase price		**$1,150**		
Refer to the chart on the next page to find the interest rate and mortgage you will use (i.e., 30-year, 6.5%), and divide monthly payment by that number.		÷ $6.32		÷
		= $181.96		=
. . . and multiply the result by 1,000 to determine the amount of house you can afford:		**$181,962**		

	15-year	30-year		15-year	30-year
3%	$6.91	$4.22	**7%**	$8.99	$6.65
3.125%	$6.97	$4.28	**7.125%**	$9.06	$6.74
3.25%	$7.03	$4.35	**7.25%**	$9.13	$6.82
3.375%	$7.09	$4.42	**7.375%**	$9.20	$6.91
3.50%	$7.15	$4.49	**7.50%**	$9.27	$6.99
3.625%	$7.21	$4.56	**7.625%**	$9.34	$7.08
3.75%	$7.27	$4.63	**7.75%**	$9.41	$7.16
3.875%	$7.33	$4.70	**7.875%**	$9.48	$7.25
4%	$7.40	$4.77	**8%**	$9.56	$7.34
4.125%	$7.46	$4.85	**8.125%**	$9.63	$7.42
4.25%	$7.52	$4.92	**8.25%**	$9.70	$7.51
4.375%	$7.59	$4.99	**8.375%**	$9.77	$7.60
4.50%	$7.65	$5.07	**8.50%**	$9.85	$7.69
4.625%	$7.71	$5.14	**8.625%**	$9.92	$7.78
4.75%	$7.78	$5.22	**8.75%**	$9.99	$7.87
4.875%	$7.84	$5.29	**8.875%**	$10.07	$7.96
5%	$7.91	$5.37	**9%**	$10.14	$8.05
5.125%	$7.97	$5.44	**9.125%**	$10.22	$8.14
5.25%	$8.04	$5.52	**9.25%**	$10.29	$8.23
5.375%	$8.10	$5.60	**9.375%**	$10.37	$8.32
5.50%	$8.17	$5.68	**9.50%**	$10.44	$8.41
5.625%	$8.24	$5.76	**9.625%**	$10.52	$8.50
5.75%	$8.30	$5.84	**9.75%**	$10.59	$8.59
5.875%	$8.37	$5.92	**9.875%**	$10.67	$8.68
6%	$8.44	$6.00	**10%**	$10.75	$8.78
6.125%	$8.51	$6.08	**10.125%**	$10.82	$8.87
6.25%	$8.57	$6.16	**10.25%**	$10.90	$8.96
6.375%	$8.64	$6.24	**10.375%**	$10.98	$9.05
6.50%	$8.71	$6.32	**10.50%**	$11.05	$9.15
6.625%	$8.78	$6.40	**10.625%**	$11.13	$9.24
6.75%	$8.85	$6.49	**10.75%**	$11.21	$9.33
6.875%	$8.92	$6.57	**10.875%**	$11.29	$9.43

Or, you can arrange to keep the interest and tax portion yourself—meaning you only pay the mortgage each month. In this case, you must remember when to pay your insurance and tax bills during the year, which means you must save for them in your spending plan, lest you face financial surprises when the bills arrive.

SHOPPING FOR A LOAN

OK, so you've determined that you want to own a house. Now comes the next big step—how to pay for it. You'll need that mortgage.

You're not likely to buy the first house you see. So there's no reason to accept the first mortgage you come across.

Lending is an ultracompetitive business, with thousands of lenders big and small scrambling every day to lend money to someone for a house purchase. Shop even for half a day and you'll undoubtedly find a rate that's cheaper and fees that are lower than the first mortgage you were offered.

In fact, you should probably shop for a loan before you shop for your home. This way you'll have no worries about the mortgage a lender will provide, and no question about what the price range you should be shopping in.

Of course, the shopping can be a chore since comparing loans is more than seeking out the lowest interest rate. Lenders also quote points and closing costs, both of which factor into the amount of money you ultimately must pay for a mortgage.

- *Points* represent up-front costs you pay to the lender to lock in a particular interest rate. Some lenders charge no points; some charge fractional points; some charge two points or more. Each point is the equivalent of 1 percent of the loan value. With a $250,000 mortgage, then, one point means you'll pay $2,500. When you pay points you essentially "buy down" the interest rate. The more points you pay, the lower the rate. Don't shy away from points just because it means more up-front costs. Over many years the lower interest rate means you will have to repay tens of thousands of dollars less than you would with a no-points loan. So if you plan on living in your house for many years, paying a point or two could save you barrels of money over time.

- *Closing costs* are fees you pay to a host of service providers, such as title and escrow companies, certain government agencies, couriers, and lawyers. Ask

SHOPPING FOR A MORTGAGE

Step 1: Call several lenders, at least a half dozen, and request today's current rate on the type of mortgages you're interested in—such as a 30-year fixed-rate conventional, for instance, or an adjustable rate mortgage, or even a balloon note. Ask each lender for multiple quotes, based on the points you might be willing to pay. (By the way, PMI, in the chart, stands for private mortgage insurance, a monthly addition to your payment a lender will generally require that you make if you put down less than 20% of the home's purchase price.)

Lender	Phone #	Loan Type (30-yr., ARM)	Rate	Points	Total Closing Costs	Total Monthly Payment	Lock-in Period	PMI Required?	Prepay Penalty?

Step 2: Using this formula, determine which lender offers the best deal. The lender with the lowest total cost for the type of mortgage you want is probably the best deal for your wallet.

		Example	Lender 1	Lender 2	Lender 3
Line 1	Mortgage Amount	$250,000			
Line 2	Points	1.25%			
Line 3	Cost of points paid (Line 1 × Line 2)	$ 3,125			
Line 4	Loan Fees	$ 800			
	Total Cost (Line 3 + Line 4)	**$ 3,925**			

each lender to provide you a list of all the fees that you will pay so that you can effectively compare the true costs of each mortgage.

Use the chart on page 77 to keep tabs on which lender offers what mortgage at what cost. Visit www.WSJ.com/BookTools to print as many copies of this chart as you need. Remember that mortgage rates change daily—sometimes several times a day—so it will be difficult to accurately compare mortgages if you gather a couple today, a few more several days from now, and some others a week or two later.

TAX SAVINGS

The great benefit of home ownership—aside from having a place to store your stuff and sleep at night—is the tax deduction you're eligible for each year.

The IRS allows you to deduct the interest portion of your mortgage payment as well as any property taxes you pay. You must itemize your taxes—that is, fill out Schedule A—to claim these deductions. The net effect means your mortgage payment isn't as costly as it appears.

Say you buy a $200,000 Average American Home, putting $40,000 down and picking up a $160,000 mortgage for 30 years at 6%. Your principal and interest payment is a little more than $959 a month. Assume property taxes are about $150 each month and insurance is another $100. Your monthly house note: $1,209.

On that particular mortgage, you'll pay over the first year about $9,547 in interest, and $1,800 in property taxes. You have a write-off, then, of $11,347 at tax time. (Each year that number changes, because tax rates change and because the amount of interest you pay grows progressively smaller; in Year 2, for instance, total interest payments amount to $9,515.) How much of that $11,347 you actually save depends on your state and federal tax rates, which you can determine by looking at the tax-rate schedules the IRS publishes at www.irs.gov (search for "Tax Rate Schedules").

Assume you and your spouse earn $100,000 combined and you file your taxes jointly. In 2005 that income was taxed at a marginal rate of 25%. Say your state taxes were 4%, so that overall you're paying 29% in taxes.

Multiply that percentage by the amount you can claim on your tax return and you have your annual tax savings. In practice it looks like this:

Tax Savings = (Deductible Interest + Property Taxes) × Tax Rate
Tax Savings = $11,347 × 0.29—or about $3,291.

On a monthly basis, that's a savings of about $274. That means the real, after tax cost of your $1,209 monthly house note is closer to $935.

MARGINAL VERSUS EFFECTIVE TAX RATES

Income-tax rates work by taxing your income at different levels as your income grows.

Assume that you and your spouse file your tax returns jointly and report $100,000 in so-called adjusted gross income, or AGI, which is essentially all of your various sources of income for the year, minus the various deductions you're eligible to claim. At $100,000, you fall into the 25% tax bracket. But that doesn't mean you owe $25,000 in taxes. Only the highest dollars of your income are taxed at the highest level, this is what's known as your *marginal tax rate.*

Your income is actually taxed at various levels along the way. So with that $100,000, the first $14,600 is taxed at 10%, the next $44,800 (or $59,400, the top end of the 15% range, minus the $14,600 that was already taxed at 10%) is taxed at 15%, and so on. Ultimately, it looks like this:

Tax Rate	Married Filing Jointly	Taxable Income	Taxes Due
10%	Up to $14,600	$14,600	$1,460
15%	$14,600 to $59,400	$44,800	$6,720
25%	$59,400 to $119,950	$40,600	$13,800
	Total	$100,000	$18,330

In all, this taxpayer would owe taxes totaling $18,330, resulting in an *effective tax rate* of 18.33%.

CALCULATING THE EQUITY IN YOUR HOME

Whether you're applying for a home-equity loan, or trying to calculate your net worth, you need to know the amount of equity you have in your house.

That calculation is simple:

CALCULATING EQUITY IN YOUR HOME

Current home value		________
Mortgage balance	−	________
Home-equity loans or lines of credit	−	________
Home equity	=	________

Home Equity	÷	**Current Home Value**	=	**Equity Ownership**
________	÷	________	=	________ %

Here's another reason to keep tabs on the equity you've accumulated: Once your equity ownership reaches 20% or more, you can request a cancellation of the private mortgage insurance you've probably been forced to carry. Known as PMI, this insurance is not for your benefit, but rather compensates the lender in case you default on your mortgage and your property doesn't fetch enough to pay off the loan balance in foreclosure.

Lenders typically wrap PMI into the cost of your monthly house note if your down payment, or your equity in the house, falls below 20%. On a $250,000 mortgage, PMI will roughly add between $104 and $208 to your monthly cost.

Once your equity tops 20% of the value of your house, your lender no longer needs the policy, though the company that services your mortgage isn't likely to ring you up to remind you of this immediately.

By law, lenders are supposed to cancel PMI when your payments have reduced your loan balance to 78% of the value of the home at the time you bought it. That, however, doesn't take into account the rising value of your home. If you bought a $200,000 home with 15% down, or $30,000, yet the value of your home rises to $215,000, well, you now have in excess of 20% equity in your house. The math: You owe $170,000 on a home worth $215,000, giving you equity of $45,000, or 20.9% of the current value of your house. Actually, the equity you own on a percentage basis is higher, since your mortgage debt will be lower than $170,000 because your monthly note includes principal payments that will have reduced the amount of money you owe.

You'll probably need to have your home appraised before the lender will agree to cancel the policy, but you'll recoup that cost of a couple hundred dollars in just a few months, and then have money for other purposes that otherwise would have gone to PMI.

TO REFINANCE OR NOT

Periodically, interest rates head lower, allowing consumers to borrow money at more affordable prices. In those moments, home owners have an opportunity to refinance their mortgage and save potentially hundreds of dollars a month and tens of thousands of dollars over the life of the mortgage.

Generally, home owners refinance for a few reasons: to lower their monthly note; to tap the accumulated equity in their home for spending on wants and needs; or to switch from one type of mortgage to another, maybe trading an adjustable-rate mortgage for a fixed-rate mortgage.

Refinancing, however, is not a cost-free proposition. You must pay various fees and closing costs on the new mortgage. You must also take into account how long you expect to live in your home. If your expected remaining time is fairly short, the savings you generate with a less-expensive mortgage might still not equal the costs of the refinancing itself. In that case, it makes more sense financially to keep your current payment, despite its loftier monthly burden. If you plan to remain in your home for many years, then refinancing to even a marginally lower-rate mortgage will ultimately save you thousands of dollars.

The simple worksheet on the next page will help you determine whether it benefits your pocketbook to refinance at currently available interest rates, or whether the mortgage you already have remains the better deal.

THE OLD COLLEGE TRY:
SAVING FOR A CHILD'S EDUCATION

The first thing to remember about paying for a child's college education is this: You don't necessarily have to pay for it—for several reasons.

- Scholarships, grants, and aid: During the 2003–4 academic year, students nationwide received more than $122 billion for college expenses, an average of about $10,500 per student. Essentially, a lot of money exists out there that you can tap into.

WHEN REFINANCING MAKES SENSE—OR NOT

Sometimes refinancing a mortgage is a great way to reduce your monthly house note. Sometimes it's not. The costs listed below are some of the major fees and expenses generally imposed on mortgages, though various lenders charge various fees that might not be listed here. Be sure to ask your lender for the laundry list of fees you will have to pay at closing, and include them in the line labeled "other." Also, use the worksheet titled "Shopping for a Mortgage" (page 77) to help determine which lenders offer you the best overall pricing for your mortgage. Visit www.WSJ.com/BookTools for copies of both.

If the break-even period extends out farther than the amount of time you expect to remain in the house, then refinancing at the currently available rates does not make sense.

Refinancing Costs	**Example**	**Your Refinancing**
Application fee	$100	
Points	$1,000	
Insurance	$750	
Legal fees	$750	
Title	$500	
Appraisal	$250	
Inspection	$100	
Recording fees	$250	
Other	$500	
Total Costs	$4,200	

Monthly Note	**Example**	**Your Refinancing**
Current payment	$1,200	
New payment	$1,020	
Monthly savings	$180	
Break-even period in months	23.33	

(Total Costs divided by Monthly savings)

- Work: There's no rule that says students can't work before and during college to help pay for or defray the costs of their own education. And they have a full working career after school to pay off student loans they can take out to cover tuition and books and such.

- Retirement: As in your own. Heartless as it might sound, saving for your years in retirement are far more important than saving every last penny for your child's college degree. As noted above, kids can work and pursue scholarships, grants, and loans to pay for school. No one will offer you scholarships and grants to live your retirement—and do you really want to work through retirement just to afford your life?

Without question, college is costly. For the 2004–5 school year, the average four-year public school cost about $11,400 for tuition and room and board. Head to a top-flight state school like the University of California, Los Angeles or the University of Michigan, and costs surge to between $17,000 and $35,000, depending on residency status. Private schools can cost $40,000 or more. And remember, those are *per-year* amounts, meaning a four-year degree can rub up against $150,000.

But if you're determined to pay for all or part of your child's college, don't let the big numbers intimidate you. People rarely pay cash for big purchases like cars and homes, and college is no different. For one thing, you'll likely be able to afford some of the expense right from your paycheck. College costs generally coincide with parents' peak earning years, so you're likely to be in better financial shape than you were when the kids were first born. You no longer have child-care costs or educational expenses, for instance, freeing up some income you can earmark for college costs.

For most parents, however, preparing for college means salting away a little money every month for many years. While there are all manner of ways to save—from CDs to savings bonds—three key savings options stand out: custodial accounts, Coverdell Education Savings Accounts, and 529 College Savings Plans. Like everything else in the personal finance world, each has its strengths and weaknesses.

Custodial accounts—also known as UGMA and UTMA accounts—allow parents, grandparents, or anyone to make an irrevocable gift of cash to a minor. Remember: This is *irrevocable;* you cannot reclaim the money once it's in the account. That will have ramifications when the child hits the age of

COMPARING THE KEY COLLEGE SAVINGS OPTIONS

Account	Pros	Cons
Custodial Accounts (Uniform Gifts to Minors Act and Uniform Transfers to Minors Act, UGMA/UTMA)	• Can save as much money as you can accumulate. • Unlimited investment choices. • Earnings are not penalized if the money is not used for educational purposes.	• Gifts are irrevocable; a child at age of majority (18 or 21) gains control of the account and can spend the money in whatever fashion, counter to your desires. • Big impact on financial aid, since half the account value is considered eligible for educational expenses. • Beneficiary cannot be changed. • No tax-incentives on withdrawals used for educational expenses.
Coverdell Education Savings Accounts	• Tax-free withdrawals if used for qualified educational expenses. • Money can be used to pay for private-school costs prior to college. • Wide array of investment choices.	• If not used for educational expenses, earnings taxed as ordinary income, and penalized an additional 10%. • Small annual contribution limits not likely to allow you to accumulate enough for college. • Limited ability to change beneficiary.
529 College Savings Plans	• Can generally save as much as $250,000 per student. • Tax-free withdrawals if used for qualified educational expenses. • Parents retain control over the assets. • Financial-aid friendly. • Beneficiary can be changed. • Account can be rolled over from one generation to another.	• Limited investment choices. • Tax advantages may expire at the end of 2010. • Prepaid version of 529 plans are not financial-aid friendly. • If not used for educational expenses, earnings taxed as ordinary income, and penalized an additional 10%.

majority—either eighteen or twenty-one, depending on the state. At that point, the child has complete say over the account and how the money is spent. That means if Junior wants to buy a Porsche instead of using the money on a pre-law degree, there's nothing you can do about it legally.

You can establish a custodial account at any brokerage firm, mutual-fund company, or bank. The key advantage: You can save as much money as you'd like. The key disadvantages: Along with losing control over the cash at a certain point, the earnings are taxed every year, depleting the amount of money you have for college costs.

Coverdell Education Savings Accounts were formerly known as Education IRAs. These allow you to save and withdraw money tax-free, so long as the dollars are used for qualified education expenses (see the chart on page 84).

The key advantages: Along with tax-free growth and withdrawals, you can tap a Coverdell to pay for a child's private schooling before college. The key disadvantage: Parents can only save $2,000 per beneficiary, per year. So that means if grandparents contribute, say, $1,500, Mom and Dad can only kick in an additional $500. Even over eighteen years of saving, $2,000 annually just isn't going to get you into the ballpark of what you're likely to need ultimately. Also, at certain income levels, parents' ability to contribute to a Coverdell account phases out. Additionally, you have a limited ability to change beneficiaries, and the money must be distributed by age thirty.

529 College Savings Plans also allow you to save and withdraw money without paying taxes if the cash is used for qualified education expenses. They're offered by state governments through financial advisors, brokerage firms, banks, and others, and with roughly $50 billion in assets in 2005 have become one of the most popular personal-finance accounts around.

The key advantages: You can save substantial amounts of money, a cumulative $250,000, likely to be plenty enough for college. You don't relinquish control of the money if the original beneficiary doesn't attend college or receives a full-ride scholarship; you can switch beneficiaries and even name yourself the beneficiary if you'd like to use the money at some point, maybe return to school in retirement. The key disadvantages: investment options are limited to generally a few select mutual funds, and the tax advantages are scheduled to expire on December 31, 2010, though with so many American families relying on the 529 plan as their college savings vehicle of choice, Congress is likely to make the tax-free status permanent.

QUALIFIED EDUCATION EXPENSE DEFINED

IRS Publication 970, which you can find at the IRS Web site, www.irs.gov, outlines what falls under the rubric of "qualified education expense." The list is short:

- Tuition and fees necessary to enroll in school.
- Expenses for special-needs services incurred by special-needs students.
- Books, supplies, and equipment necessary to participate in classes. Though the IRS publication doesn't spell this out, in some cases "equipment" can mean a laptop computer, for instance, if the school or a particular degree requires that students be able to access the school's Internet site for various educational reasons.
- Room and board.

Any other expenses are not covered.

HOW MUCH TO SAVE?

That's the $64,000 question—and $64,000 probably won't be enough.

The worksheet on page 88 will help you determine how much you need to save, but before you attack it there are a few things to recognize (visit www.WSJ.com/BookTools for an interactive version of this worksheet):

1. Don't assume that expensive schools are automatically out of your price range. That's the biggest mistake parents make. The amount of financial aid a student qualifies for is relative to the cost of the chosen school. School financial-aid officers look at a family's so-called demonstrated financial need, defined as the cost of attending the school minus the family's expected financial contribution. So, for instance, if your family can afford just $2,000 a year, yet your child wants to attend a $30,000-a-year school, your demonstrated financial need is $28,000—and that's the figure the aid officers work toward, though that doesn't necessarily mean they'll be able to come up with the entire amount. Still, the point is that you'll qualify for more money at an

expensive school than at a much cheaper community college simply because the need is greater.

2. Don't assume your assets disqualify you from receiving aid. While assets are certainly a part of the federal financial-aid formulas, those formulas are largely structured around current income. The idea is that you can draw upon your income on a pay-as-you-go approach while your child is enrolled in school. Moreover, those formulas recognize that parents must save for other obligations, namely retirement. Also, most merit scholarships don't take into account a family's financial situation. They're based on, well, merit. And merit doesn't mean academic merit only; numerous organizations offer cash based on musical, artistic, and athletic prowess, as well as civic activities within a community. The Henkel Corporation, the Avon, Ohio, maker of Duck-brand duct tape, even awards $5,000 every year to the high school couple that fashions the nattiest prom attire entirely from duct tape.

   The college-funding world is filled with millions of scholarships. FastWeb.com lists roughly 600,000 on its continuously updated online database. Sign up for free, plug in a host of educational, demographic, athletic, and civic information and FastWeb finds all the scholarships a student might be eligible for. And as new ones come in, the Web site alerts you via email. Also, SLM Corporation, commonly known as Sallie Mae, offers a free-scholarship database (College Answer, at collegeanswer.com) with information on about 2.4 million scholarships worth more than a combined $14 billion annually.

WARNING: Do not pay any company that guarantees for a fee of a few hundred dollars that it can find college financial aid for you. It is a scam. Such companies gather basic family financial data and dump it into a Free Application for Federal Student Aid—a so-called FAFSA form that all schools use to calculate aid eligibility—and then obtain for you the same $1,000 you could have obtained filling out the FAFSA form yourself. If you have trouble filling out the form, ask a college aid officer; they'll never charge you a penny.

3. Don't forget about state scholarship programs. Numerous states have in place scholarship programs for local high-school kids who enroll in state-based schools, both public and private. These scholarships generally cover tuition, mandatory fees, and, often, a book allowance. They don't typically cover room and board.

   Information on the various state scholarship programs is available online at each state's higher-education agency Web site. The U.S. Department of Education, meanwhile, operates a database of state aid agencies that lists

COLLEGE-COST AND SAVINGS CALCULATOR

Future Costs of College Calculation

STEP 1

Current College Costs $20,000

Determine the current cost of college at a school you think your child is likely to attend, public or private. Visit that school's Web site for the current year's cost of tuition and books—and room and board, if your child will live on campus.

STEP 2

Cost Escalation Factor 2.720

College costs have historically risen by about 8% a year. To determine how much a year of college is likely to cost in the future, determine how many years remain until your child's freshman classes begin, and find the Cost Factor associated with that year in the chart below.

YEARS BEFORE ENROLLMENT	ANNUAL RATE OF RETURN				
	3%	5%	8%	10%	12%
1	1.0300	1.0500	1.0800	1.1000	1.1200
2	1.0609	1.1025	1.1664	1.2100	1.2544
3	1.0927	1.1576	1.2597	1.3310	1.4049
4	1.1255	1.2155	1.3605	1.4641	1.5735
5	1.1593	1.2763	1.4693	1.6105	1.7623
6	1.1941	1.3401	1.5869	1.7716	1.9738
7	1.2299	1.4071	1.7138	1.9487	2.2107
8	1.2668	1.4775	1.8509	2.1436	2.4760
9	1.3048	1.5513	1.9990	2.3579	2.7731
10	1.3439	1.6289	2.1589	2.5937	3.1058
11	1.3842	1.7103	2.3316	2.8531	3.4785
12	1.4258	1.7959	2.5182	3.1384	3.8960
13	1.4685	1.8856	2.7196	3.4523	4.3635
14	1.5126	1.9799	2.9372	3.7975	4.8871
15	1.5580	2.0789	3.1722	4.1772	5.4736
16	1.6047	2.1829	3.4259	4.5950	6.1304
17	1.6528	2.2920	3.7000	5.0545	6.8660
18	1.7024	2.4066	3.9960	5.5599	7.6900
19	1.7535	2.5270	4.3157	6.1159	8.6128
20	1.8061	2.6533	4.6610	6.7275	9.6463

STEP 3

Future College Costs $54,392

Multiply Step 1 by Step 2 to determine the cost of school in your child's freshman year.

STEP 4

Total 4-Year Costs $245,096

College-cost price escalation doesn't stop the moment your child enrolls. Each year will be more expensive than the previous. In the chart below, choose the annual rate of college-cost inflation you expect, then multiply the corresponding factor by the Future College Costs in Step 3.

ANNUAL RATE OF RETURN				
3%	5%	8%	10%	12%
4.1836	4.3101	4.5061	4.6410	4.7793

Monthly Savings Needs Calculation

STEP 5

Current Savings $5,000

Enter the amount of money you've already saved for your child's college costs—even if that number is zero.

Future Value $13,598

Assuming the number is greater than $0, you'll need to calculate the estimated value of the account by the time your child enrolls. Find in the chart below where the rate of return you expect intersects with the number of years before enrollment, and multiply that number by your Current Savings.

YEARS BEFORE ENROLLMENT	ANNUAL RATE OF RETURN				
	3%	5%	8%	10%	12%
1	1.0300	1.0500	1.0800	1.1000	1.1200
2	1.0609	1.1025	1.1664	1.2100	1.2544
3	1.0927	1.1576	1.2597	1.3310	1.4049
4	1.1255	1.2155	1.3605	1.4641	1.5735
5	1.1593	1.2763	1.4693	1.6105	1.7623
6	1.1941	1.3401	1.5869	1.7716	1.9738
7	1.2299	1.4071	1.7138	1.9487	2.2107
8	1.2668	1.4775	1.8509	2.1436	2.4760
9	1.3048	1.5513	1.9990	2.3579	2.7731
10	1.3439	1.6289	2.1589	2.5937	3.1058
11	1.3842	1.7103	2.3316	2.8531	3.4785
12	1.4258	1.7959	2.5182	3.1384	3.8960
13	1.4685	1.8856	2.7196	3.4523	4.3635
14	1.5126	1.9799	2.9372	3.7975	4.8871
15	1.5580	2.0789	3.1722	4.1772	5.4736
16	1.6047	2.1829	3.4259	4.5950	6.1304
17	1.6528	2.2920	3.7000	5.0545	6.8660
18	1.7024	2.4066	3.9960	5.5599	7.6900
19	1.7535	2.5270	4.3157	6.1159	8.6128
20	1.8061	2.6533	4.6610	6.7275	9.6463

(continued)

STEP 6

Unmet Need $231,498

Subtract the Future Value in Step 5 from the total four-year costs in Step 4. This represents how many additional dollars you still need to accumulate to reach your goal. Your goal does not necessarily have to be the entire four-year cost of college. It can be any amount you establish as your goal, since you or your kids can pursue loans, grants, and scholarships to cover some of the costs.

STEP 7

Savings Factor 0.00366

Find in the chart below the Savings Factor that equates with the number of years you have to save before the freshman year begins and the annual rate of return you expect on your investments. The shorter the number of years before enrolling, the more conservative you should be—meaning a heavier weighting toward lower-return, but safer, bond investments—since you do not want a bear market in stocks to sharply shrink your savings just as your child is set to enroll. The longer the number of years, the more aggressive you can be.

YEARS BEFORE ENROLLMENT	ANNUAL RATE OF RETURN				
	3%	5%	8%	10%	12%
1	0.08219	0.08144	0.08032	0.07958	0.07885
2	0.04048	0.03970	0.03856	0.03781	0.03707
3	0.02658	0.02580	0.02467	0.02393	0.02321
4	0.01963	0.01886	0.01775	0.01703	0.01633
5	0.01547	0.01470	0.01361	0.01291	0.01224
6	0.01269	0.01194	0.01087	0.01019	0.00955
7	0.01071	0.00997	0.00892	0.00827	0.00765
8	0.00923	0.00849	0.00747	0.00684	0.00625
9	0.00808	0.00735	0.00635	0.00575	0.00518
10	0.00716	0.00644	0.00547	0.00488	0.00435
11	0.00640	0.00570	0.00475	0.00419	0.00368
12	0.00578	0.00508	0.00416	0.00362	0.00313
13	0.00525	0.00456	0.00366	0.00315	0.00269
14	0.00480	0.00412	0.00325	0.00275	0.00231
15	0.00441	0.00374	0.00289	0.00241	0.00200
16	0.00406	0.00341	0.00258	0.00213	0.00174
17	0.00376	0.00312	0.00232	0.00188	0.00151
18	0.00350	0.00286	0.00208	0.00167	0.00132
19	0.00326	0.00264	0.00188	0.00148	0.00115
20	0.00305	0.00243	0.00170	0.00132	0.00101

STEP 8

Monthly Savings Needs $847

Multiply Step 6 by Step 7. This represents the amount of money you need to save starting today to reach your unmet need by the time your child enrolls.

contact information. The site is located at studentaid.ed.gov; look for the state-aid link under the "Funding" tab.

4. Don't overlook the financial benefit of Advanced Placement tests. Many students take AP tests and use the credits to place out of low-level college courses, but then ultimately pursue the same number of credits. But you don't have to do it that way if money is tight. High school students can earn enough credits through AP tests to enter college as sophomores, easily saving $10,000 or more. That's good value, given that an AP test costs about $82, and local high schools will often pay that fee.

   AP tests are offered once a year, usually in the spring, but many universities also offer College Level Examination Program tests, so-called CLEP tests. You generally have to foot the $75 fee yourself, but there's no set testing date; just call the school, ask if they offer CLEP tests, and sign up to take the ones you want.

   After you determine the costs, you might be wondering how to invest your savings based on the age of your child right now. This chart will give you a feel for how you should allocate your money:

HOW TO ALLOCATE YOUR CHILD'S COLLEGE SAVINGS

	Age				
	0–3	4–7	8–11	12–15	16–18
Stocks	55%	45%	35%	20%	0%
Bonds	20%	40%	55%	75%	70%
Int'l. Stocks	25%	15%	10%	0%	0%
Cash	0%	0%	0%	5%	30%

BUYING A CAR

Cars are expensive. Ten thousand dollars for the most basic models. Tens of thousands for the hot-selling models and the popular sport utility vehicles. Fifty thousand or more for luxury sedans, high-end roadsters, and imported sports cars.

For many consumers, such price tags mean one of two options: borrow money to buy what you can afford, or rely on a lease to put your hands on the wheel of what you really want to drive but can't afford to buy using an auto loan. Either way, you're financing the transaction and that has repercussions on your wallet.

Many financial pros argue that financing a car makes no sense because the asset depreciates the instant you drive it off the lot. It's not like you're borrowing money to buy a house that, over time, will likely increase in value and which provides valuable tax breaks. There's merit to that argument, but it is shortsighted and Draconian. Cars are, in most American cities, a necessity. And anyone who thinks American drivers are simply going to own the least expensive ride they can find is living in a financial Neverland.

So this take on automotive finance is built on the premise that you're going to buy a car, even if you don't have every penny saved, and you're probably not going to rush out and logically buy the cheapest, most utilitarian vehicle you can find. That's just the reality of life.

If you're going to buy, then recognize this: It's not always cheapest to pay cash. Sometimes, the financial impact on your life is less onerous if you finance the purchase. This is typically the case when automakers provide special-incentive, low-rate financing. In those situations it can pay to do the math shown on the following worksheet, since borrowing money to buy a car instead of paying all cash means less money out of your pocket in the end.

TO BUY OR FINANCE YOUR NEW CAR

CASH PURCHASE			Example		Your Car
Line 1	Negotiated sales price		$25,000		
Interest income lost on cash used for purchase					
Line 2	Divide Negotiated sales price by 1,000	25			
Line 3	Savings rate	3.50%			
Line 4	Number of years financed (How many months would you finance, if you had financed instead? Should match Line 21 below.)	48			
Line 5	Savings Factor (Insert value from Savings Factor chart where interest rate intersects Number of months financed.)	1150.04			
Line 6	Multiply Line 2 by Line 5	$28,751			
Line 7	Interest income lost by using cash to buy a car (Line 6 − Line 1)	$3,751			
Line 8	Your income-tax rate	27%			
Line 9	Taxes on interest income (Line 7 × Line 8)	$1,013			
Line 10	Total income forsaken (Line 7 − Line 9)	$2,738			
		Total Cash Cost (Line 1 + Line 10)	**$27,738**		

SAVINGS FACTOR CHART

NUMBER OF MONTHS FINANCED	INTEREST RATE 1.5%	2.0%	2.5%	3.0%	3.5%	4.0%	4.5%	5.0%
12	1015.10	1020.18	1025.29	1030.42	1035.57	1040.74	1045.94	1051.16
24	1030.44	1040.78	1051.22	1061.76	1072.40	1083.14	1093.99	1104.94
36	1046.00	1061.78	1077.80	1094.05	1110.54	1127.27	1144.25	1161.47
48	1061.80	1083.21	1105.06	1127.33	1150.04	1173.20	1196.81	1220.90
60	1077.83	1105.08	1133.00	1161.62	1190.94	1221.00	1251.80	1283.36
72	1094.11	1127.38	1161.65	1196.95	1233.30	1270.74	1309.30	1349.02

(continued)

FINANCED PURCHASE		Example		Your Car	
Line 11	Negotiated sales price	$25,000			
Line 12	Down payment		$2,500		
Interest income lost on cash used for purchase					
Line 13	Divide down payment by 1,000	2.5			
Line 14	Multiply Line 13 by Line 5	$2,875			
Line 15	Interest income lost by using down payment (Line 14 − Line 12)	$375			
Line 16	Taxes on interest income (Line 15 × Line 8)	$101			
Line 17	Total income forsaken (Line 15 − Line 16)		$274		
Monthly payments					
Line 18	Financed amount (Line 11 − Line 12)	$22,500			
Line 19	Divide financed amount by 1,000	22.5			
Line 20	Interest rate on car loan	2.90%			
Line 21	Number of months financed	48			
Line 22	Money factor (Insert value from chart where Interest Rate intersects Number of months financed.)	$22.09			
Line 23	Monthly payment (Line 22 × Line 19)	$497.03			
Line 24	Total of all payments (Line 23 × Line 21)		$23,857		
	Total Finance Cost (Line 12 + Line 17 + Line 24)		**$26,631**		

MONEY FACTOR CHART

NUMBER OF MONTHS FINANCED	INTEREST RATE							
	0.9%	**1.9%**	**2.9%**	**3.9%**	**4.9%**	**5.9%**	**6.9%**	**7.9%**
12	83.74	84.19	84.65	85.10	85.56	86.02	86.48	86.94
24	42.06	42.50	42.94	43.38	43.83	44.28	44.73	45.18
36	28.16	28.60	29.04	29.48	29.93	30.38	30.83	31.29
48	21.22	21.65	22.09	22.53	22.98	23.44	23.90	24.37
60	17.05	17.48	17.92	18.37	18.83	19.29	19.75	20.23
72	14.27	14.71	15.15	15.60	16.06	16.53	17.00	17.48

By the same token, it doesn't always make sense to jump at the ultralow-rate financing, even the 0% financing, that automakers use to lure you into the showroom. Consider, for instance, that at one point in 2005 the Ford Motor Company offered buyers of its economy-priced Focus an incentive: $2,000 cash back or 0% financing over 36 months. But pay attention to the "or" in the middle of that sentence: Car companies typically don't offer the low-rate financing *and* the rebate. Choose to use the carmaker's money for free through 0% financing, and the dealer isn't likely to cut you any slack on the sales price. Look how this real-life situation actually plays out:

Assuming you put in $2,000 of your own money as a down payment, that 2005 Focus at 0% financing meant a monthly note of $312 for three years. But take the $2,000 rebate, along with your original $2,000 down payment, and pay 2.9% for the same 36 months (realistic at the time), your note is just $268—a monthly savings of $44, or nearly $1,600 over the life of the loan.

The message: Run the numbers before you run to the dealer. Financing at 0% isn't always as cheap as it sounds.

THE INS AND OUTS OF AUTO LEASES

Before you rush out to lease that top-of-the-line Jaguar that seems so enticingly affordable at $250 a month for the next 17 years, take the time to understand the factors that determine a monthly lease payment so that you're not carjacked by an auto dealer using your lack of insiders' knowledge against you.

The first question to ask yourself is whether it makes sense to lease in the first place, or whether you're better off buying. So before you jump into a lease, jump into the worksheet on page 97 to determine what's best for your pocketbook.

Assuming you've determined you want to pursue a lease, the most important number to know is the depreciated value of the vehicle you want. That value, spread across the number of months involved in your lease, determines your monthly payments. Just as with buying a car outright, many of the components of an auto lease are negotiable, so you want to know the numbers the dealer is relying on to come up with the depreciated value and, ultimately, the monthly note.

Three numbers establish everything: capitalized cost, residual value, and the so-called money factor. These three factors plugged into the worksheet will

SOMETIMES ZERO MEANS MORE THAN NOTHING

PURCHASE WITH REBATE	Example		Your Car	
Negotiated sales price	$13,230			
Manufacturer's rebate	$2,000			
Adjusted cost	$11,230			
Down payment		$2,000		
Net cost	$9,230			
Monthly payment (2.9% for 36 months)	$268			
Total of all monthly payments		$9,648		
Total Cost of Purchase with Rebate		**$11,648**		

0% FINANCING	Example		Your Costs	
Negotiated sales price	$13,230			
Manufacturer's rebate	$0			
Adjusted cost	$13,230			
Down Payment		$2,000		
Net cost	$11,230			
Monthly payment (0.0% for 36 months)	$312			
Total of all monthly payments		$11,230		
Total Cost of 0% Financing		**$13,230**		
Monthly savings (Difference between monthly notes)		$44		
Savings over life of the loan (Monthly savings × loan term)		$1,582		

BUYING VERSUS LEASING A VEHICLE

Leasing might seem cheaper because the monthly note is more affordable. But financing a car can actually be easier on your wallet in the end. This example assumes the same $30,000 car is either leased or financed for 48 months. The interest rate on the financed vehicle is 5.25%, an available rate on new-car loans in mid-2005. All "Leasing Costs" information will come from a dealer, or from the worksheet "Calculating the Best Car-Lease Deal" on page 101. The information noted below is actual lease data from mid-2005.

LEASING COSTS	Example	Your Car
Security payment	$5,000	
Total of all monthly payments ($396 for 48 months)	$19,008	
End-of-lease payment*	$1,500	
Total Leasing Costs	**$25,508**	

TRADITIONAL FINANCING COSTS		Example		Your Car	
Line 1	Down payment/trade-in/rebate		$5,000		
Line 2	Amount financed	$25,000			
Line 3	Divide financed amount by 1,000	25			
Line 4	Interest rate on car loan	5.25%			
Line 5	Number of months financed	48			
Line 6	Money Factor (insert value from Money Factor chart where Interest Rate intersects Number of months financed)	23.1427			
Line 7	Monthly payment (Line 3 × Line 6)	$578.57			
Line 8	Total of all monthly payments (Line 7 × Line 5)		$27,771		
Line 9	Estimated car value at end of loan		($12,000)		
	Total Financing Costs (Line 1 + Line 8 + Line 9)		**$20,771**		

* For excessive wear, vehicle damage, excessive mileage. You must look at the lease details before signing to determine what these costs could potentially amount to. This example assumes you drive 10,000 extra miles over the life of the lease, at $0.15 per mile.

MONEY FACTOR CHART

NUMBER OF MONTHS FINANCED	INTEREST RATE							
	4.00%	4.25%	4.50%	4.75%	5.00%	5.25%	5.50%	5.75%
12	85.1499	85.2642	85.3785	85.4930	85.6075	85.7221	85.8368	85.9516
24	43.4249	43.5363	43.6478	43.7595	43.8714	43.9834	44.0957	44.2080
36	29.5240	29.6353	29.7469	29.8588	29.9709	30.0833	30.1959	30.3088
48	22.5791	22.6911	22.8035	22.9162	23.0293	23.1427	23.2565	23.3706
60	18.4165	18.5296	18.6430	18.7569	18.8712	18.9860	19.1012	19.2168
72	15.6452	65.8177	17.1739	60.3448	18.7763	55.5924	20.4179	51.5286
	6.00%	6.25%	6.50%	6.75%	7.00%	7.25%	7.50%	7.75%
12	86.0664	86.1814	86.2964	86.4115	86.5267	86.6420	86.7574	86.8729
24	44.3206	44.4333	44.5463	44.6593	44.7726	44.8860	44.9996	45.1134
36	30.4219	30.5353	30.6490	30.7629	30.8771	30.9915	31.1062	31.2212
48	23.4850	23.5998	23.7150	23.8304	23.9462	24.0624	24.1789	24.2957
60	19.3328	19.4493	19.5661	19.6835	19.8012	19.9194	20.0379	20.1570
72	16.5729	63.1380	18.7432	56.3645	20.8691	51.1464	22.9034	47.1109
	8.00%	8.25%	8.50%	8.75%	9.00%	9.25%	9.50%	9.75%
12	86.9884	87.1041	87.2198	87.3356	87.4515	87.5675	87.6835	87.7997
24	45.2273	45.3414	45.4557	45.5701	45.6847	45.7995	45.9145	46.0296
36	31.3364	31.4518	31.5675	31.6835	31.7997	31.9162	32.0329	32.1499
48	24.4129	24.5304	24.6483	24.7665	24.8850	25.0039	25.1231	25.2427
60	20.2764	20.3963	20.5165	20.6372	20.7584	20.8799	21.0019	21.1242
72	17.5332	60.7367	20.3167	53.1353	22.8879	47.8265	25.1981	44.0469

allow you to effectively comparison-shop the auto leases different dealers are offering.

Capitalized cost is the agreed-upon sales price, which you can negotiate just as you would the sticker price of any car you buy.

Residual value is what the dealer expects the car's value will be when you return it at the end of the lease term. You don't have direct control over this, but many auto Web sites list which cars retain their value the best. That gives you some control in choosing cars that retain their value. The greater the residual value, the smaller the depreciated value and, thus, the more affordable your monthly note.

The *money factor* is the cost of borrowing, leasing's equivalent of the interest rate attached to a conventional loan.

TURNING A MONEY FACTOR INTO AN INTEREST RATE

One of the more confusing components to auto leases is the money factor, the numerical value the auto dealer plugs in to determine how much your lease payment will be after you agree on the cost of the car. The money factor basically serves as the interest rate would in a conventional loan—it is the cost of borrowing.

Calculating the interest-rate equivalent of the money factor requires nothing more than a little math: Multiply the money factor by 24.

Interest Rate = Money Factor × 24

__________ = __________ × 24

So, if a dealer tells you (more likely you'll have to ask) that the money factor on a particular lease is 0.03854, well you can whip out a pencil or calculator and quickly determine that you're paying the equivalent of a 9.25% loan rate.

This is a prime reason it pays to do your homework before you walk into a showroom: If you know that interest rates on car loans at your local credit union or bank are 7%, there's no reason in the world why you'd want to pay substantially more with an auto lease. (By the way, always carry a calculator, notepad, and pencil when shopping for a car lease. That way you can do all your calculations and show the salesman you know what's what.)

REMEMBER: The capitalized cost and the money factor are both negotiable. That means you have the power to push for a lower sticker price on the car you want, and a cost of borrowing that is in line with what you would get through conventional financing. Those efforts will save you thousands of dollars over the life of the lease.

COMPARING LEASES

Don't assume the lease you're offered at one dealer is pretty much the same as you'd get at another dealer. Just as you'd shop two or more showrooms when buying a car outright, you should shop for the best deal you can negotiate when leasing a car or truck.

The worksheet on page 101 will make that process easier. Plug in the capitalized cost, residual value, and money factor, and you can calculate your monthly lease payment to determine which dealer is offering you an acceptable deal.

Some last notes of caution with auto leases:

- In most states, so-called lemon laws don't apply to leased vehicles. These laws mandate that a carmaker provide a remedy for consumers who buy vehicles that fail to meet certain quality and performance standards—such as a car that repeatedly is in the shop for the same repair issue.
- All four tires must match if you return the car to the dealer at the end of the lease. If they don't, you'll pay for a set of new tires to replace the mismatched tires.
- If you exceed the cumulative mileage limit of typically between 10,000 and 15,000 miles annually, you'll pay a fee of 10 to 20 cents for every mile over the limit. This alone generally makes leases a bad deal for drivers who put lots of miles on their cars during the year.
- Insurance can be a bear. Some lenders require that you carry a $0 deductible on your comprehensive and collision coverage, which raises your rates dramatically. And, if you total the car, your insurance won't pay for lease payments, taxes, or fees you'll still owe. That means you'll need "gap insurance"

CALCULATING THE BEST CAR-LEASE DEAL

Use this worksheet to compare the lease offers that various dealers present. By negotiating the Capitalized Cost and the Money Factor, you will see immediately how that impacts your monthly payment.

		Example	Dealer #1	Dealer #2	Dealer #3
Line 1	**Capitalized Cost** (The negotiated sticker price)	$30,000			
Line 2	**Downpayment, Trade In, Rebates**	($5,000)	–	–	–
Line 3	**Total Capitalized Cost** (Line 1 – Line 2)	$25,000			
Line 4	**Residual Value**	($13,000)	–	–	–
Line 5	**Depreciation** (Line 3 – Line 4)	$12,000			
Line 6	**Length of Lease (months)**	48	÷	÷	÷
Line 7	**Monthly Depreciation** (Line 5 ÷ Line 6)	$250			
Line 8	**New Capitalized Cost plus Residual Value** (Line 3 + Line 4)	$38,000			
Line 9	**Money Factor** (Obtain from dealer)	0.00385	×	×	×
Line 10	**Lease Company Fee** (Line 8 × Line 9)	$146.30			
Line 11	**Monthly Depreciation** (Line 7)	$250	+	+	+
	Total Monthly Payment (Line 10 + Line 11)	$396.30			

to pay off the lease and the residual value of the car. That adds to the overall monthly operating costs.

- Finally, leases are legal contracts that can be difficult, if not impossible, to get out of if you ultimately decide you can't afford the notes or don't like the car. You're likely to be hit with sizable fees if you back out of the contract. Do not enter into a lease lightly, or just because it helps you afford a car you otherwise couldn't buy with your current finances.

CHAPTER 5

Be Prepared—It's Not Just a Motto for the Boy Scouts

There's one last aspect of building your financial base that you need to pursue: preparing yourself for any potential emergency that might arise, everything from planning for the day you lose your wallet to keeping track of all your financial accounts to knowing where the important paperwork is in the event of a tragedy or death.

THE WALLET REGISTER

To borrow an advertising line, What's in your wallet?

All of us carry some sort of billfold, pocketbook, coin purse, money clip, or wallet to corral our currency, a few family photos, a driver's license, likely a few too many credit cards, a health-insurance card, an ATM or debit card, and, maybe, our Social Security card.

Now, just imagine losing your wallet, or having it stolen. If either has ever happened to you, you know the instantaneous panic that sets in. OK, so you lose the cash that's in your wallet; you're mad, but that's not so bad—unless, of course, you were traveling overseas and lost all the money you brought on vacation. You undoubtedly feel a tug of nostalgic sadness at losing keepsakes like the photos or, maybe, that lucky dollar your son gave you when he was five. But what really pumps the adrenaline is that fear that some ne'er-do-well is suddenly living the good life on your MasterCard. You've got to get to a phone pronto to cancel your cards—wait, what are the phone numbers to MasterCard and American Express? What's my Visa number? And, which cards did I have in there anyway?

Keeping tabs on the inventory in your wallet is a form of financial planning that can pay off if ever your wallet goes missing. In that event, you'll quickly know what you were carrying around and who to call to cancel and replace credit cards.

Thus, this wallet register on the next page.

Fill in the worksheet on page 105 and keep it in a safe place, preferably a lockbox or family safe at home. You can keep a second copy in a bank safe-deposit box so that if anything happens to you, whoever is charged with handling your affairs will know what you might have had in your wallet that needs to be addressed in some fashion. But remember: You'll want fast access to this data if your wallet vanishes, and there's no promise that will happen only during banking hours. So keep a copy in a secure spot at home. Visit www.WSJ.com/BookTools to print copies of the register.

FINANCIAL ACCOUNTS

Chances are you have more than a checking or savings account. You might have a certificate of deposit and probably a 401(k) or similar retirement plan from work. You might have opened a traditional IRA years ago, or maybe a rollover IRA, or maybe a Roth IRA. Maybe you do a bit of consulting or freelance work on the side and you've been wise enough to pump a bit of that income into a Keogh account or a SEP-IRA. Possibly you own U.S. Treasurys through Treasury Direct.gov or have a full-service brokerage account at Merrill Lynch and a discount brokerage account at Charles Schwab. Do you have a life-insurance policy? What about an annuity?

As with the inventory in your wallet, you need to keep track of the various financial accounts you have. And unless you're a finance junkie checking in on these accounts every day or two online, you might have a tough time remembering all the details like account numbers and Web addresses and passwords and such. A safe bet is that if you're married your spouse probably doesn't keep up with all—maybe even most—of these accounts, either.

All this information is important data, though, particularly in a situation

THE WALLET REGISTER

Driver's license number ______________________________

DMV phone number ______________________________

Use this grid to record information on credit cards, department-store and gas charge cards, and ATM and debit cards. Don't forget corporate credit cards. And keep this document safe; it contains very sensitive data.

Card	Issuer	Card Number	Phone Number

Check off which cards you routinely carry in your wallet, and jot down the account number and contact phone number in the spaces below each.

☐ Airline Frequent-Flyer
No. ______________________
Ph. ______________________

☐ Auto Insurance
No. ______________________
Ph. ______________________

☐ Auto Club
No. ______________________
Ph. ______________________

☐ Health Insurance
No. ______________________
Ph. ______________________

☐ Dental Insurance
No. ______________________
Ph. ______________________

☐ Social Security
No. ______________________
Ph. ______________________

☐ Long-Distance Card
No. ______________________
Ph. ______________________

☐ Library Card
No. ______________________
Ph. ______________________

☐ Movie Rental
No. ______________________
Ph. ______________________

☐ Other
No. ______________________
Ph. ______________________

where something happens to you, and a spouse or family member needs to know where to find the family's assets quickly.

What you need is a personal-finance record keeper to catalog your financial existence. Keep the worksheet on page 107 very secure, since it lists all the data necessary to tap into each account. Some security pros might blanch at putting on paper what is essentially the key to unlocking your entire financial life, but the reality is that a spouse or a parent or a child or a sibling is going to have to know what accounts exist, where they're located, and how to access them if you die or become incapacitated to such a degree that you can't help yourself. There is some level of risk involved in keeping this list, but that risk can be mitigated with a little common sense.

First, keep the list where no one can get to it except you and the people who need access to it in an emergency. This doesn't mean keeping it on your computer—particularly a laptop—since those can be compromised. Similarly, don't keep it in a portable lockbox at home. Those, too, can be fairly easily infiltrated.

Instead, keep this list in a home safe or, better yet, in a safe-deposit box at the bank. Just make sure that your spouse, your partner, your parents, your lawyer, or whoever it is that might ultimately need to see this document knows where it resides and has access to it in times of necessity. The last thing anyone needs in an emergency is the frustration of not knowing where to find crucial financial information.

SAFE-DEPOSIT BOXES

Most folks stash in their safe-deposit box just about everything of value or perceived value or importance, be it the family-heirloom jewelry (a good selection for a safe-deposit box) or a will (a bad selection).

But don't consider a safe-deposit box a dumping ground for every life and family-finance document that hits your mailbox. Some papers certainly deserve to be stored there; others most assuredly do not.

To make life easier on you and your family, keep family documents in the correct location, and keep a list that specifies what document is where.

This is a list you do *not* want to keep in the safe-deposit box. Because if it's there, the people you designate to manage your affairs in an emergency or in the event you die or become incapacitated—a spouse, parents, sibling, your children—may not be able to get into your box until a lawyer files the legal papers

THE FAMILY FINANCE PERSONAL RECORD KEEPER

Checking/Savings Accounts & Certificates of Deposit

Name of institution ______________________ Account #: ______________________

Account type: ______________________ Web site: ______________________

Physical address: ______________________ Login: ______________________

______________________ Password: ______________________

Phone: ______________________ Document location: ______________________

Name of institution ______________________ Account #: ______________________

Account type: ______________________ Web site: ______________________

Physical address: ______________________ Login: ______________________

______________________ Password: ______________________

Phone: ______________________ Document location: ______________________

Name of institution ______________________ Account #: ______________________

Account type: ______________________ Web site: ______________________

Physical address: ______________________ Login: ______________________

______________________ Password: ______________________

Phone: ______________________ Document location: ______________________

Name of institution ______________________ Account #: ______________________

Account type: ______________________ Web site: ______________________

Physical address: ______________________ Login: ______________________

______________________ Password: ______________________

Phone: ______________________ Document location: ______________________

(continued)

Brokerage & Retirement Accounts

Name of institution ______________________ Account #: ______________________

Account type: ______________________ Web site: ______________________

Physical address: ______________________ Login: ______________________

______________________ Password: ______________________

Phone: ______________________ Document location: ______________________

Name of institution ______________________ Account #: ______________________

Account type: ______________________ Web site: ______________________

Physical address: ______________________ Login: ______________________

______________________ Password: ______________________

Phone: ______________________ Document location: ______________________

Name of institution ______________________ Account #: ______________________

Account type: ______________________ Web site: ______________________

Physical address: ______________________ Login: ______________________

______________________ Password: ______________________

Phone: ______________________ Document location: ______________________

Name of institution ______________________ Account #: ______________________

Account type: ______________________ Web site: ______________________

Physical address: ______________________ Login: ______________________

______________________ Password: ______________________

Phone: ______________________ Document location: ______________________

Stocks & Bonds (held personally)

Asset: ______________________ # of shares/bonds: ______________
Document location: ______________________ Cusip #: ______________

Asset: ______________________ # of shares/bonds: ______________
Document location: ______________________ Cusip #: ______________

Asset: ______________________ # of shares/bonds: ______________
Document location: ______________________ Cusip #: ______________

Insurance Policies

Insurer: ______________________ Policy #: ______________
Policy type: Home Life Auto Umbrella Other Web site: ______________
Physical address: ______________________ Login: ______________
______________________ Password: ______________
Contract value: ______________ Beneficiary: ______________
Phone: ______________ Document location: ______________

• •

Insurer: ______________________ Policy #: ______________
Policy type: Home Life Auto Umbrella Other Web site: ______________
Physical address: ______________________ Login: ______________
______________________ Password: ______________
Contract value: ______________ Beneficiary: ______________
Phone: ______________ Document location: ______________

• •

Insurer: ______________________ Policy #: ______________
Policy type: Home Life Auto Umbrella Other Web site: ______________
Physical address: ______________________ Login: ______________
______________________ Password: ______________
Contract value: ______________ Beneficiary: ______________
Phone: ______________ Document location: ______________

(continued)

Insurance Policies *(continued)*

Insurer: ______________________ Policy #: ______________________

Policy type: Home Life Auto Umbrella Other Web site: ______________________

Physical address: ______________________ Login: ______________________

______________________ Password: ______________________

Contract value: ______________________ Beneficiary: ______________________

Phone: ______________________ Document location: ______________________

Insurer: ______________________ Policy #: ______________________

Policy type: Home Life Auto Umbrella Other Web site: ______________________

Physical address: ______________________ Login: ______________________

______________________ Password: ______________________

Contract value: ______________________ Beneficiary: ______________________

Phone: ______________________ Document location: ______________________

Insurer: ______________________ Policy #: ______________________

Annuity type: Varied Fixed Web site: ______________________

Physical address: ______________________ Login: ______________________

______________________ Password: ______________________

Contract value: ______________________ Beneficiary: ______________________

Phone: ______________________ Document location: ______________________

Safe-deposit Box

Bank: ______________________ Bank address: ______________________

Box # ______________________ ______________________

Location of box key: ______________________

Home Safe/Lockbox

Location: ______________________

Combination/location of keys: ______________________

necessary. Note that while laws vary, banks typically require a death certificate before they'll grant permission for a nonowner to remove contents from a safe-deposit box, and that could take a few days to obtain—though some banks may grant you access to at least photocopy some documents.

Instead, keep the family-documents worksheet on page 112 in a lockbox at home. Since this document does not list passwords and financial-account numbers, its utility is narrow to would-be scofflaws. Once again, make sure that the appropriate people in your life know that this document exists and where to find it.

As a general rule, documents you don't have reason to reference often, or which you wouldn't need in an emergency, are fodder for a safe-deposit box. Many of these can be replaced if they're lost. This would include:

- Birth and death certificates
- Marriage certificates
- Divorce decrees
- Baptismal records
- Property deeds
- Automobile titles
- Stock and bond certificates (although, if you have a full-service broker, and you want to keep the certificates in your name, you might want to keep them on file there. Your broker will need them fairly quickly if you or your heirs want to sell those securities).
- Home-improvement records. Heirs will need these to document the cost basis of your home. Unlike the other papers listed here, these documents are usually receipts and they exist in only one place; they can't be replaced, so you need to protect them.

The documents listed on page 113 are ones you should *not* keep in a safe-deposit box. Many of these you, a spouse, or other family members will likely need to access quickly in an emergency. Instead, keep these in a safe or fireproof lockbox hidden in your home. While these, too, can be replaced, you don't want to subject yourself or family members to the added stress of having to find a duplicate copy quickly or at odd hours. Visit www.WSJ.com/BookTools to print as many copies as you need.

LOCATION OF KEY FAMILY DOCUMENTS

Note: Letters in parentheses, such as (sb), denote where each document is best kept, though your situation may dictate something different.

(sb) = Safe-deposit box; (lb) = Fireproof lockbox or home safe

Documents	Location
Birth certificate(s)	(sb)
Death certificate(s)	(sb)
Marriage certificate(s)	(sb)
Divorce decree(s)	(sb)
Child custody/adoption decree(s)	(sb)
Social Security card(s)	(lb)
Passport(s)	(lb)
Estate documents	
Will(s)	(lb)
Living will(s)	(lb)
Trust(s)	(lb)
Power(s) of attorney	(lb)
Funeral arrangement documents	(lb)
Deeds and titles to property	
Real estate	(sb)
Auto(s)	(sb)
Other	
Stock & bond certificates (not held at a brokerage)	(sb)
Insurance policies	
Home	(lb)
Auto(s)	(lb)
Life	(lb)
Umbrella	(lb)
Health	(lb)
Long-term care	(lb)
Disability	(lb)
Other	
Home improvement records/receipts	(sb)

- Wills

- Trusts

- Power-of-attorney

- Passport

- Life-insurance policies and annuity contracts. You could keep these in a safe-deposit box; however; if you do, keep in the lock-box a copy of the policy number, the name on the policy, the name of the insurer and information, which is often a Social Security number. Insurers generally don't require the policy itself to pay on the contract, but they will need all the identifying data, so it's best to have that handy in the event that accessing the safe-deposit box is inconvenient or impossible at a given moment.

In a digital age, when scanning all manner of documents takes just seconds, storing the important papers electronically on a computer seems a great way to keep them all handy and instantly accessible at any hour of the day or night.

That, though, isn't the best idea. For one, computers can be stolen or hacked, and all your vital information can be used to raid your finances. Moreover, when it comes to many of these documents, you can't just print them out and use them. Birth certificates, auto titles, and others all need that raised seal indicating that the document is the original. Scanning does serve one useful purpose: It makes replacing the original substantially easier, since your scanned copy will have all the relevant information on it.

PART II

BUILDING YOUR ASSETS

CHAPTER 6

INVESTING

If building your financial base is all about the present, building your assets is all about the future. And the future promises to be an expensive place.

There's college to think about for any kids you might have and, of course, the tremendous costs of retirement to finance once you stop working for a living and start living on what you worked for all your life. That's what building your assets is all about. After all, if you only had today to worry about, you could spend what you earn and be fine. But you have your future ahead of you. There are cars to buy, at tens of thousands of dollars each. There are houses costing at least $100,000, likely more, to buy. You face college costs if you have children and plan to pay for their education—and that's tens of thousands to hundreds of thousands each, depending on where the kids enroll.

And then there's your retirement. Mind-boggling it is to think you could have in retirement possibly as many years as you had in the workforce. That's decades to survive only on what you've saved and what you receive each month from Social Security, assuming Social Security survives in its current form by the time you retire. That long amount of time means you could need more than $1 million to live a lifestyle similar to what you lived before retirement.

To the great consternation of many, success in saving for each of those expenses is largely about investing.

Part of the reason people shy away from investing is because they face such a wide and sometimes confusing array of possibilities: precious metals, options, futures, commodities, exchange-traded funds, and annuities. The list goes on. But average, individual investors need go no more exotic than the three basic investments—stocks, bonds, and mutual funds. In all honesty, most people are well suited to sticking exclusively with mutual funds, since with those you'll be able to build an instantly diversified portfolio of various types of assets efficiently and cost effectively.

Investing isn't voodoo. It isn't scary. It isn't hard. It isn't about luck. It has nothing to do with "hot tips" or "inside information." Though "asset allocation" might sound like so much jibberish, you'll soon learn just how simple it can be to distribute your money—known as allocating your assets—between various stocks, bonds, or mutual funds. After all, millions of individual investors of all ages successfully manage their own investments, and they do so even though they spend their 9-to-5 hours working as mail carriers and electricians and nurses and pilots and ferryboat captains and lawyers and . . . the point is that you don't need to be a money maven to survive Wall Street. In fact, you don't even have to think about Wall Street; many very good mutual funds are based well away from New York City, in places like Houston, Texas, and St. Paul, Minnesota. So don't be intimidated by the term *Wall Street.*

The truth is, the definition of "investor" is someone who invests money—simple as that. And you don't really even need much investment knowledge or experience to be an investor. All you really need to do is decide that you want to invest in something as simple and straightforward as a Standard & Poor's 500-stock index fund in your 401(k) plan. Suddenly, you're an investor—and you don't even need to know what Standard & Poor's is or what stocks comprise the 500.

All you need is the gumption to get going and a little guidance on what you're doing, how to pick what to own, and knowledge about where you're ultimately headed. All of that starts with the basics—your net worth.

DETERMINING YOUR NET WORTH

You've probably seen at some point those thermometer-shaped signs around town that depict how far along some particular blood drive or money drive has progressed. Well, that's your net worth—a temperature gauge of your finances. It pinpoints where you are at any given point in your life, information necessary to figure out how much you need to save to get to where you think you want to go. If your goal is the metaphorical finish line, then your net worth is your current location on the track. Visit www.WSJ.com/BookTools for an interactive version of the worksheet on the next page.

CALCULATING YOUR NET WORTH

ASSETS

Cash		$
Savings/money market		
Checking		
Certificates of deposit		
Other savings-based assets (savings bonds, etc.)		
Life insurance, cash value		
Annuities, surrender value		
Investments		
Brokerage account		
Mutual-fund account		
Stocks/bonds held personally		
Investment real estate		
Investments total		
Retirement accounts		
Keogh		
SEP-IRA		
Traditional/Rollover IRA		
401(k), 403(b), etc.		
Profit sharing		
Pension plan balance		
Retirement accounts total		
Market value of primary home		
Market value of autos		
Jewelry/precious metals/gemstones		
Collectibles		
Furnishings/Art		
Other assets		
Total Assets		$

LIABILITIES

Mortgage(s)	
Auto loan balance(s)	
Credit-card balance(s)	
Student loans	
Back taxes owed	
Home-equity loan/line of credit	
Investment debt (margin)	
Other debt owed	
Total Liabilities	
Net Worth (total assets – total liabilities)	$

In basic terms, your net worth is a measurement of how much you're worth if you add up all the assets you own and subtract all the debts you owe. The formula looks like this:

Net Worth = Total Assets – Total Liabilities

________ = ________ – ________

With assets of, say, $500,000 and liabilities of $300,000, you have a net worth of $200,000.

This calculation forms the basis of many measurements of who you are financially. Banks want to know this stuff when you take out a loan; mortgage companies want to know this when you buy a home. You need to know what it is from time to time just to make sure you're on track toward your financial goal.

Plan on calculating your net worth once a year, maybe around the beginning of each new year, so that you can gauge your progress toward your personal finish line, wherever that is. Use the worksheet on the previous page and update it as your life progresses.

RATING YOUR TOLERANCE FOR RISK

Before you set foot on Wall Street, you have one exercise you must undertake: assessing your personal tolerance for the ebbs and flows that continually move through stocks and bonds and just about any asset you can imagine. In other words: What's your tolerance for risk?

When it comes to investing, the word *risk* flies around like a nettlesome gnat—it's everywhere. It's part of the disclosure documents you sign to open a brokerage account. It's part of the research Wall Street brokerage firms pump out. It's inherent in any mutual fund you buy.

But what exactly is risk?

In simple terms it's the possibility that you can lose all or part of the principal you invest in some particular asset. As an investor, you must be certain that you can handle the degree of risk each individual investment harbors, and they all harbor some level of risk. For instance, Treasury bonds. They're considered the safest investment in the world because the principal you invest and the interest you are due are backed by the full faith and credit of the United States government, which isn't likely to default on its debt.

Yet that doesn't mean Treasury securities carry no risk. They certainly do. While you'll never lose money if you hold your Treasury until it matures, the value of the Treasury bonds, bills, or notes that you own can—and do—fall in value based on broader interest rates and economic movements. That means if you sell before the security matures, you might get back less than you originally invested. That defines risk.

Some risks are greater than others. Treasurys are less risky than municipal bonds, which are less risky than corporate bonds, which are less risky than blue-chip stocks, which are less risky than start-up technology stocks, and so on. That continuum looks something like this:

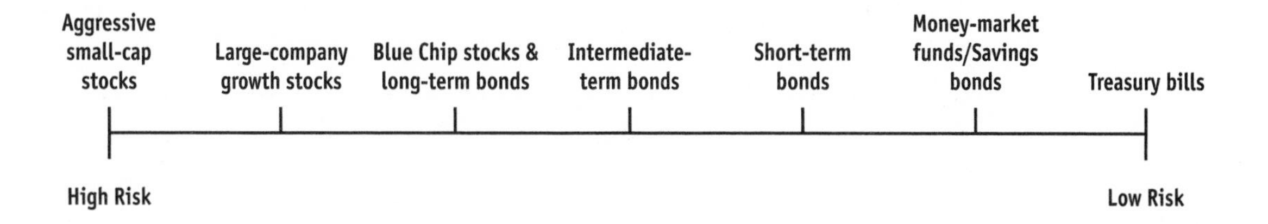

To succeed as an investor, you must know where you fall on the risk spectrum in terms of your investment objective. Are you seeking growth of your investments, meaning you can live with the high degree of volatility they exhibit in return for long-term appreciation? Or are you more comfortable just to preserve your capital because you can't stomach the thought of losing all or a part of your investment in a down market? Here's what the investment-objective continuum looks like:

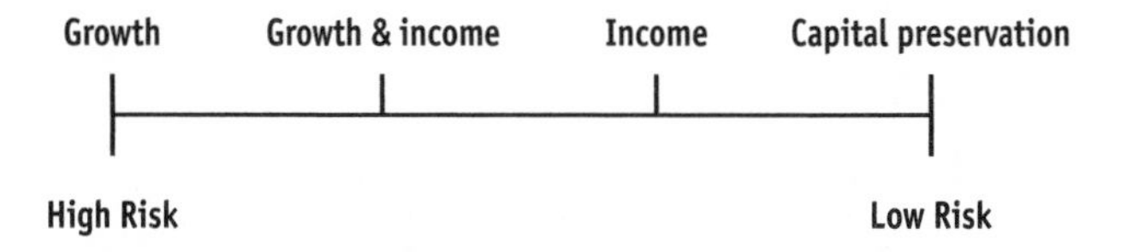

During bull markets investors forget risk exists because stocks only know one direction—up. In bear markets investors pay myopic attention to risk, sure that anything they buy is certain to sink. Both of those are precisely backward, since the height of a bull market generally represents the riskiest moments on Wall Street, while the depths of a bear market often present the least risky opportunities. Investor reaction happens this way time and again, however, because behaviorally speaking, people are irrational when it comes to money and risk. Consider this: Someone offers you a sure $50, or on the flip of a coin the possibility of winning $100 or winning nothing. What do you do? Research shows that you're likely to take the $50. Conversely, assume someone penalizes you $50 from the start, and then offers you a coin flip to recover the loss or lose $100. This time, you're much more likely to take the coin flip.

Here's the catch: Each situation is statistically identical. Yet humans tend to view the possibility of recouping a loss, even if it means a potentially greater loss, as far more important than the possibility of a greater gain.

The trick for any investor, then, is to understand risk and to know your own tolerance for risk, so that no matter what market conditions exist at any given moment, you can comfortably manage the losses that could materialize in your portfolio without panic. Because when you rush to sell in emotional moments, you lock in a decision that in more logical moments you probably would not make. That can assure an unnecessary loss or cut short an even larger potential gain.

The worksheet on the following page, excerpted from a *Wall Street Journal* article that ran in mid-2000, just after the beloved bull market of the late 1990s cracked, poses a series of questions to help you gauge where you fall on the risk spectrum. It's only eight questions long, but it's backed by empirical studies. Think about what answers truly fit your personality; don't just pick the answer that you think is going to put you into a certain category that you assume you should fall into. Be thoughtful with your answers and you might be surprised at the type of investor you really are. Visit www.WSJ.com/BookTools to print copies of this worksheet.

No matter what type of investor you are, the worst thing you can do is swing for the home runs with every investment you make. Wall Street at times can seem a land of easy riches, but believing you can turn every investment into immediate wealth by picking stocks that only go up is a fool's gamble. Though this has been said many times before, the clichés are sometimes right: Slow and steady wins the race.

SHORT TERM? LONG TERM? SOMETHING IN BETWEEN?

Before we get to the point where you open a brokerage account or start managing the money in your 401(k), you need to know a little bit about time horizons.

HOW MUCH RISK CAN YOU TOLERATE?

Answer these questions, then score yourself below:

1. Choose the statement that best describes your interest in an investment program:

a. My primary aim is to achieve high long-term return in the value of my portfolio, even if that means accepting some significant short-term swings in value.

b. My primary interest is in stable growth in the value of my portfolio, even if that means somewhat lower returns over time.

c. I attach equal value to maximizing long-term returns and minimizing fluctuations in value.

2. How important are these factors when you decide to purchase a stock or mutual fund?:

	Very Important	Somewhat Important	Not at All Important
a. Short-term potential for the price to appreciate.	A	B	C
b. Long-term potential for the price to appreciate.	A	B	C
c. If a stock, the potential that the company will be acquired or taken over.	A	B	C
d. Gain or loss in the price over the past six months.	A	B	C
e. Gain or loss in the price over the past five years.	A	B	C
f. Stock was recommended by a friend or coworker.	A	B	C
g. Risk that the price could drop.	A	B	C
h. Potential that the investment will pay dividends.	A	B	C

3. Would you put $5,000 of your assets into an investment with:

	Yes	No
a. a 70% chance of doubling your money (to $10,000) and a 30% chance of losing the entire $5,000?	________	________
b. an 80% chance of doubling to $10,000 and a 20% chance of losing the entire $5,000?	________	________
c. a 60% chance of doubling to $10,000 and a 40% chance of losing the entire $5,000?	________	________

(continued)

4. Suppose you have a choice between two mutual funds, both of which are broadly diversified into 6 asset classes (e.g., stocks, bonds, real estate, etc.). These charts show the changes in value over the past 12 months for the assets in each portfolio. In which portfolio do you prefer to invest?

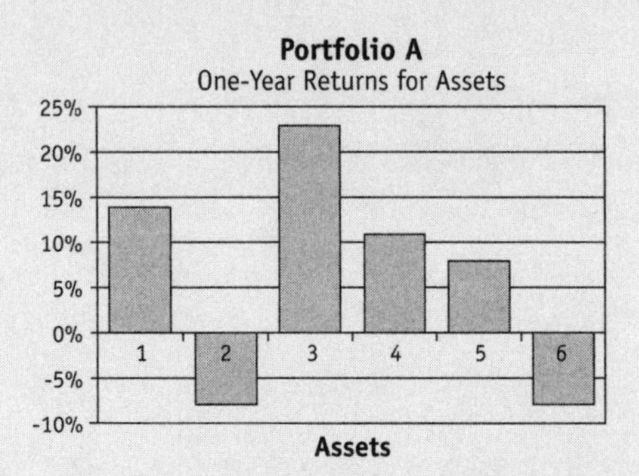

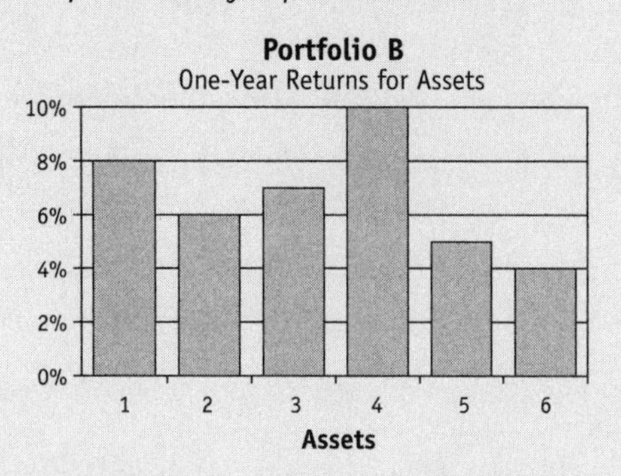

5. Assume that you have made an investment that has dropped in value by $2,000 and you're faced with the following choice (circle one option only):
   - **a.** Sell and take the immediate loss (a 100% chance of loss).
   - **b.** Hold onto it with a 50% chance of recouping the $2,000 and a 50% chance of losing an additional $2,000.
   - **c.** No preference.

6. Assume you have recently invested $10,000 in a stock, and that the value of the stock has dropped 15% in one week. You can find no reason for this decline, and the broader market has not dipped accordingly. Which of the following actions would you most likely take (circle one option only):
   - **a.** Buy more.
   - **b.** Sell all your holdings immediately and put the money into a less volatile investment.
   - **c.** Sell half your holdings immediately and put that money elsewhere.
   - **d.** Wait for the price to recover and then sell all your holdings in the stock.
   - **e.** Do nothing. (Occasional dips in prices are to be expected.)

7. The following charts show quarterly performance of two equity funds over the past two years. Which do you prefer to invest in?

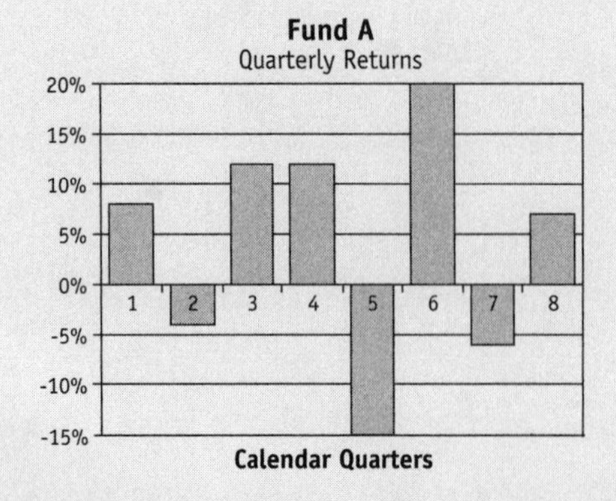

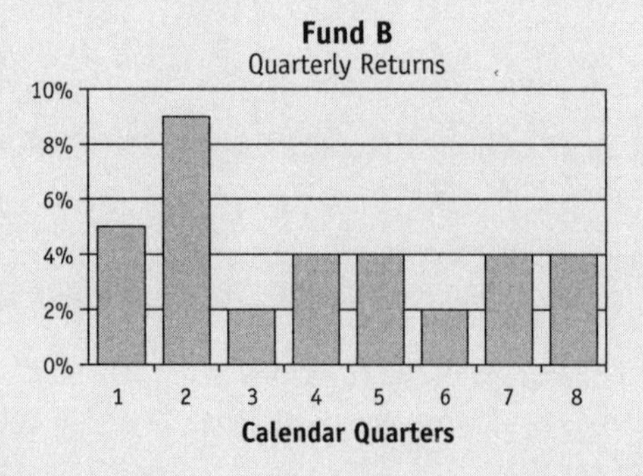

8. As an investor in stock and bond markets, how would you rate your degree of experience relative to other individual investors (circle one option only):

a. Extremely experienced.

b. More than average experience.

c. Average experience.

d. Less than average experience.

e. Little or no experience.

Scoring

1. **a, 15; b, 0; c, 7**
2. **For each question:**
a: A, 0; B, 1; C, 2
b through e: A, 2; B, 1; C, 0
f through h: A, 0; B, 1; C, 2
3. **For each question:**
a through c: Yes, 5; No, 0
4. **A, 10; B, 0**
5. **a, 0; b, 10; c, 10**
6. **a, 15; b, 0; c, 5; d, 0; e, 10**
7. **A, 10; B, 0**
8. **a, 20; b, 15; c, 10; d, 5; e, 0**

Score	Suitable Investments*
0–11	Avoid risk! Open a money-market account—or buy a bigger mattress.
12–23	Gentlemen, and ladies, prefer bonds, and are most at home with high-grade corporate and government bonds of an intermediate duration.
34–55	You're still a bond buyer. But you're willing to live a little closer to the edge with interest-only U.S. Treasury STRIPS.
56–77	Mix it up. Convertible bonds and stocks are to your liking. But safer utilities and large blue-chip stocks are as risky as you go. Real-estate investment trusts fit, too.
78–99	Stock up on stocks. At the low end, you're comfortable with larger-value stocks; at the high end, riskier midcap and growth stocks work.
100+	Viva Las Vegas, baby! Place your bets on risky Internet stocks and new-technology issues. Risks are high, but so are the potential payoffs.

** Based upon an analysis of the volatility of 75 various bond and stock indexes, applied to investment horizons of between 10 and 15 years.*

In other words, you need to know the differences between investing for the short term, the long term, or the intermediate term. Each serves a different purpose and each has its own set of risks that you must pay attention to, or you risk losing money you can't afford to or not gaining as much as you otherwise might.

There's nothing at all difficult here; it's really simple: The shorter your investment horizon, the more conservative you want to be. The longer your investment horizon, the more risk-tolerant you can be. The rationale is equally simple: Short-term investing is for money you expect to need in the next year or three for an expense such as a down payment on a new house or upcoming college expenses; you don't want short-term money in risky assets, like stocks, that could lose value and leave you short of the necessary money you need. Conversely, if you're investing for the long term—say, a retirement that is twenty years away—you most certainly don't want all your cash in conservative investments, like savings bonds and certificates of deposit, since those won't keep pace with inflation, leaving you well short of the amount of money you'll need to live on later.

This chart provides a sense of what types of investments match each time frame:

LET'S DO THE TIME WARP

Time Frame	Appropriate Investments
Short-term: typically 3 years or less	Cash, certificates of deposit up to 3 years in duration, Treasury bills and Treasury notes up to 3 years in duration, money-market accounts/funds.
Intermediate-term: typically 3 to 10 years	Cash, CDs of 5 years or more, Treasury notes up to 10 years in duration, high-grade corporate and municipal bonds, conservative stocks such as stable utilities, dividend-paying Blue Chips, and real-estate investment trusts.
Long-term: typically 10 years or more	Blue Chip stocks mixed with aggressive small-cap stocks and international stocks. A smaller focus on corporate bonds and Treasurys exceeding 10 years in duration, high-yield junk-bond funds.

COMPOUNDING: THE MOST POWERFUL FORCE IN THE UNIVERSE

Albert Einstein once claimed that "the most powerful force in the universe is compound interest." It's easy to see why that's so: all the money you put to work earns interest, and all that interest earns interest, and all the interest that the interest earns earns interest. And so on, every day, every month, every year. That's huge power.

Interest compounds in cash accounts like checking and CDs. With stocks, annual returns compound, so that if you start with $1,000 and it earns, on average, 10% a year compounded (the average annual return for the market going back to the 1920s) then after five years you'd have nearly $1,611. Of course, to be fair about it all, stock market returns don't move in an average annual fashion each year—meaning they don't go up 10% a year. Some years the market is up 18%, some years it's down 7%. You might invest an entire lifetime and never actually see a year in which stocks were up exactly 10%, though if you smooth out all those ebbs and flows over your investment career, you would have earned the equivalent of 10% annually.

The best way to really grasp compounding is to see it in action:

THE POWER OF COMPOUNDING $1,000

Years	5%	10%	15%
1	$1,050	$1,100	$1,150
2	$1,103	$1,210	$1,323
3	$1,158	$1,331	$1,521
4	$1,216	$1,464	$1,749
5	$1,276	$1,611	$2,011
6	$1,340	$1,772	$2,313
7	$1,407	$1,949	$2,660
8	$1,477	$2,144	$3,059
9	$1,551	$2,358	$3,518
10	$1,629	$2,594	$4,046
11	$1,710	$2,853	$4,652
12	$1,796	$3,138	$5,350
13	$1,886	$3,452	$6,153
14	$1,980	$3,797	$7,076
15	$2,079	$4,177	$8,137

Just remember: There is no average annual year! So don't assume you're going to earn some particular return in any given year.

FIRST THINGS FIRST

For movie buffs, there's a line in *Coming to America* in which Eddie Murphy's character announces that "one cannot fly into flying. One must first learn to walk." The same sentiment holds true with investing. Before you dash off to make your fortune on Wall Street, you need a foundation.

That foundation begins with building the emergency fund discussed earlier in the workbook. Your emergency savings is the buffer you need to protect your family in times of crisis or urgency and, as such, is the most important building block to achieving financial security.

From there you want to save for retirement, either through a company-sponsored retirement savings plan such as a 401(k), or, if you don't have access to such a plan at work, then through an IRA. With this step you're building financial security for the future, a time when all the money you have is all the money you'll get to live out your days.

Recognize that you can do these first two at the same time. You can save for retirement with each paycheck and build your emergency account. If, for instance, you determine you can save $200 a month, then split that down the middle, saving $100 in your retirement fund and putting the other $100 in your emergency savings. Keep that up until you've built your emergency account to the appropriate size, then funnel the full $200 into your retirement plan.

Saving for a house should be third on your list—assuming you ultimately want to be a home owner. Buying a home isn't necessarily for investment purposes, since you purchase a house primarily for shelter. Still, a home is typically the largest purchase anyone makes and, thus, is typically the largest asset most people own, and over time real-estate prices tend to escalate alongside the rate of inflation, roughly 3% a year on average historically. That will serve you well later in life, when you can either take out a reverse mortgage on your house to create income to live off of in retirement, or if you opt to sell your home and downsize to a smaller house, in which case you'll have leftover profits that can go a long way toward affording your life in retirement. Moreover, because of the tax breaks you get from home ownership—the ability to write off the mortgage interest and property taxes you pay—the government is helping you buy your house. That's a good deal. So, saving for, and ultimately buying, a home is the third leg of building financial security.

The final leg is investing outside your retirement plan. Here's the thing: You don't want all of your investment money in various retirement accounts. Remember, retirement accounts generally forbid you from touching your money until you're fifty-nine and a half, unless you pay a penalty. You don't want to be in a situation where you need access to cash for whatever reason but can't get at it without losing part of it to a penalty because you're not old enough to tap into your retirement account yet.

For that reason, you want money invested in a brokerage or mutual fund account. This is money that will grow over time at a rate faster than inflation, and that you will have access to—without penalty—for whatever purpose that arises in life. All of which means you need to know about brokerage accounts, what types exist, and which one is best for your circumstances.

BROKERAGE-FIRM BASICS

You don't just go to the corner market to buy shares of stock or mutual funds. You don't ring up the New York Stock Exchange and tell the operator you're looking to buy some IBM and a little Pfizer. You go through a brokerage firm of some sort.

What type of firm you choose depends on what type of investor you are—a do-it-yourself investor or one who needs or wants a little hand-holding. Either way, the options are numerous. You have traditional, full-service brokers such as Merrill Lynch, Morgan Stanley, A.G. Edwards, Raymond James, Prudential, and others; and you have discount, online brokers such as Fidelity, Charles Schwab, E*Trade, BrownCo, Scottrade, and more.

Both types of brokerage firms do essentially the same thing—execute your orders to buy and sell stocks, bonds, and mutual funds. However, each appeals to a different sort of investor. What type of account you'll want depends entirely on what you need from a brokerage firm—investment advice and other services, or access to inexpensive trading.

Full-Service

With these firms you're hiring a broker to execute trades for you, to call you with stock recommendations, and to provide in-house research produced by the brokerage firm's team of research analysts.

Full-service accounts are right for investors who need advice choosing individual investments, want access to the proprietary research, need help creating a portfolio, or have special needs for managing an account. However, you generally need a fairly substantial account, $50,000 to $100,000 or more, since many full-service firms don't want their brokers spending time trying to squeeze revenue out of relatively small accounts. If you want or need full-service amenities but don't have such deep pockets, consider a smaller or regional full-service firm, such as A.G. Edwards, Raymond James, or Edward Jones. They're more likely to want your business.

No matter which you choose, however, you will pay more for the added handholding. Full-service firms charge fees based on two basic platforms: commission-based and fee-based.

- *Commission-based:* You pay a commission for each transaction you or your broker initiates, and those commissions can be $75 to $150 each. Commission-based accounts are best for investors who do not trade a lot, but who want all the various services a brokerage firm offers. These accounts are not right for investors who trade frequently; the commissions will amount to a hefty sum. But beware: the biggest knock against commission-based accounts is that they're ripe for abuse by dishonest brokers. Since commissions are paid only when a transaction is initiated, brokers have been known to "churn" these accounts, meaning they trade frequently, often without the account owner's consent, to create a commission for themselves. Churning is illegal.
- *Fee-based:* With these accounts you pay a flat fee each year that covers just about everything, including all transactions, no matter how often you trade. The annual fee, deducted from your account quarterly, typically ranges between 1% and 2% of the assets you have on deposit in the account. The size of the fees depends on your assets-under-management, or how much money you have on deposit with the firm. As your account grows, the size of the charge typically decreases. You might pay about 2% a year, or $2,000, if you have $100,000 on deposit, but only 1%, or $10,000, if you have $1 million.

Brokerage firms push these accounts over commission-based accounts because they get paid no matter what you do, even if you do nothing, and no matter if your account is up or down for the year. Generally speaking, fee-based accounts align a broker's interest with yours, since the broker's pay increases only when your account value increases.

If you're not an active trader or don't require lots of services, however, fee-based accounts can be a waste of money, since you end up paying for services you're not using. Brokerage firms are supposed to monitor your account to ensure that you are in an appropriate account; if you don't trade frequently, the firm should steer you into a commission-based account where your annual costs would be much less.

Discount Firm

These firms are Internet-based and geared toward do-it-yourself investors who make their own investment decisions, who don't want unsolicited phone calls pitching 100 shares of some flea-bitten company, and who want to execute their trades themselves. Basically, discounters are providers of utilitarian trade-execution services, and their key draw is price: commissions can be as low as $1.95, plus ½ cent per share. By and large, most of the big, well-known discount firms—such as Charles Schwab, Fidelity, and E*Trade—charge between $10 and $15 per trade.

Though you can call a toll-free number and trade over the phone, you don't deal with brokers, and a discount firm's employees do not work on commission. Nor do these firms employ research analysts to track and issue "buy," "sell," or "hold" recommendations on individual companies—although Schwab does issue recommendations based on a school-like grading system of A, B, C, D, and F.

While discount firms began as no-frills investment shops providing basic trade executions, in recent years almost all of them have begun to resemble in some fashion the full-service brokerage houses. The breadth of products they offer now extends well beyond stocks, bonds, and mutual funds and into options, certificates of deposit, annuities, life insurance, and so on. They offer college- and retirement-planning services, provide checking accounts and credit cards, and in many cases have tag-teamed with a full-service firm or two to offer clients online access to stock-market research reports. Moreover, discounters offer an abundance of stock and mutual-fund screening capabilities, as well as news alerts and even electronic bill-payment services. Some will even manage your portfolio, so long as it's at least $50,000. They do charge additional fees for this, typically ranging between 0.25% and about 1% of assets, though that fee scale is much lower than you'd find at a full-service firm.

Because of the cost savings, discounters are the best option for investors comfortable with managing their own account, doing their own research, or who don't trade frequently. Then again, if you do trade frequently, discounters are still a better option, since many specialty online firms provide very fast, trader-oriented Web sites, allowing you to trade directly in the market instead of routing your orders through a middleman, the route taken by most traditional stock transactions. Moreover, they offer steep discounts on commissions for frequent traders.

WALL STREET IN WORDS AND FORMULAS

Like lawyers speaking legalese, investors have their own patois that, unless you're in on the game, can sound, if not foreign, at least like something that requires a decoder ring to decipher.

In truth, the words of Wall Street are easy to understand. And you do need a working knowledge of them, if for no other reason, to at least grasp what financial professionals are telling you when they're providing investment services. In other situations they'll help you better understand what the market pundits jabber about on the business news shows, they'll help you better analyze the individual investments you might be interested in, or help you slip effortlessly into a stock-market conversation at the next cocktail party.

There are a ton of these words and phrases that the Street relies on when speaking the language of finance. You don't need to worry about the vast majority of them unless you want to be a committed stock investor. And if you do, there are very good books that specifically focus on those intricacies, including *The Wall Street Journal Complete Money and Investing Guidebook*. For the average person, however, there are a few basic concepts with which you at least want to be familiar:

For instance, *P/E ratio*. This term is bandied about in reference to just about every stock ever mentioned. This is the ubiquitous price-to-earning ratio, a very simple-to-derive measure of how expensive a particular stock is relative to the company's earnings. A stock's price is nothing more than a reflection of how dearly or cheaply investors value the underlying company's ability to earn profits—the primary reason any company goes into business, and the primary reason an investor wants to own shares of stock.

In general, companies with high P/E ratios are those that investors expect will continue to report robustly growing earnings, also known as net income or profit. Companies with low P/E ratios have muted growth expectations.

The formula to calculate the P/E is

P/E = Current Price ÷ Latest Four Quarters of Earnings (Price ÷ Earnings)

So, if a company's stock price trades for $20 and the company has earned in the most recent 12 months $1.25 per share—and we'll explain "per share earnings" in a moment—then it has a P/E ratio of 16 (20 ÷ 1.25 = 16).

Since that number by itself doesn't really say much, investors traditionally look at the P/E in comparison to a company's historical P/E range. If this same company historically trades in a range of 8 to 12 and it's now at 16, well the shares might be overvalued at the moment. Conversely, if the historical range is 20 to 25, then the shares may represent good value.

Net Profit Margin

The net profit margin flows directly from the proverbial bottom line because net income is typically the last—or bottom—line on a company's quarterly and annual income statements. Expressed as a percentage, this represents how efficiently a company has turned sales into profits after paying all the costs of business, such as salaries, production expenses, marketing, taxes, and the like.

Net profit margins are all over the map, depending upon the company and the industry. Many technology-intensive companies such as software makers and pharmaceutical firms boast of very healthy margins near 20% and above. That means 20 cents of every dollar in sales flows through to net profits, the earnings, which ultimately drives the stock's price. Other companies, such as those in low-tech, commodity businesses such as grocery stores, have margins of just 1% or 2% or so. This doesn't make them lousy businesses; that's just the nature of their industry. As with many investment measures, net profit margins are best examined in comparison to a company's history and in comparison to the industry in which that company operates.

The formula:

Net Profit Margin = Net Income ÷ Net Sales

Both "net income" and "net sales" are found on the "income statement," sometimes called a statement of earnings.

Yield

When you own certain stocks and bonds, you earn income in the form of dividend payments (stocks) and interest payments (bonds). Those payments, expressed as a percentage of the current price of the stock or bond, represent the yield, which is always expressed on an annualized basis.

Here's the formula:

Yield = Annual Income ÷ Current Price

So, if a mythical company that trades for $20 a share pays you $1 per share in annual dividend payments, you're earning a yield of 5% (1 ÷ 20 = .05).

Book Value

Remember the discussion earlier about calculating your net worth? Well, book value is a company's net worth; it represents the remaining cash value if the company sold off every asset and paid off every debt. This is often expressed as a per-share value, such as a book value of $13 a share.

The formula:

Book Value = Shareholders' Equity ÷ Total Outstanding Shares

You will find "shareholders' equity" and "total outstanding shares" on a company's balance sheet.

WARNING: Book value can be overstated or understated, depending upon all manner of factors—innocuous and malevolent—that companies employ. But in general, companies that trade below their book value are often seen as bargains on the theory that you could dismantle the company and create more value than the stock is currently worth. Conversely, companies whose book value is substantially above the share price—multiples of, say, five and above—are very pricey. But as with the P/E ratio, you need to know the historic range to understand the current book value in context.

PEG Ratio

This measures a company's P/E against its growth rate, the "G" in the PEG ratio. The theory: Companies whose earnings growth rate is bigger than the stock's P/E ratio may represent a bargain. If earnings are growing faster than investors are giving the company credit for (and remember that a P/E ratio is the market's estimation of the value of a company's earnings), then it stands to reason that the stock price ultimately will move higher to catch up to the earnings growth.

On the other hand, if the earnings growth rate is well ahead of the P/E, then you have an indication that investors are pricing perfection into the stock, and any perceived or real slip-up could send the shares somersaulting southward.

The formula:

PEG = P/E Ratio ÷ Growth Rate

You already know how to calculate the P/E. For the growth rate you can use one of two numbers—historic or expected. To use historic, calculate a company's year-over-year earnings growth, meaning look at the most recent earnings compared to the earnings from the same quarter a year earlier.

That formula:

growth rate = (current quarter's earnings − year-ago earnings) ÷ year-ago earnings

Or, you can go to Morningstar (at www.morningstar.com), plug in a stock symbol, and under the "Key Ratios" link find the "Growth Rates" tab that will reveal a variety of short- and long-term earnings growth rates.

If you want to use expected earnings, you'll need to find the rate at which Wall Street analysts expect a company's earnings to grow. You can find that online at Yahoo! Finance (at finance.yahoo.com), under the "Analyst Estimates" link. Yahoo! even shows the PEG ratio—if you don't want to calculate it yourself.

CALCULATING YOUR RATE OF RETURN

What did I earn?

Investors ask themselves that question each time they sell an investment. The calculations necessary to reach the answer differ depending upon whether you own a stock, a bond, or a mutual fund. Here's how to calculate your return on investment:

CALCULATING YOUR RATE OF RETURN

TO CALCULATE YOUR RATE OF RETURN ON A STOCK OR BOND:

$$\text{Rate of Return} = \frac{(\text{Total Sales Proceeds} - \text{Total Purchase Price}) + \text{Income}}{\text{Total Purchase Price}}$$

So, let's say you buy 100 shares of LMNOP Widget Technology for $10 a share, and you pay a commission of $15 to your discount broker. Your total purchase price is $1,015: [(100 × $10) + $15].

And then you sell those same 100 shares two years later for $16.75 apiece, and pay another $15 in commission, for total sales proceeds of $1,660: [(100 × $16.75) − $15]. Along the way, you received eight quarterly dividend payments of $0.08 per share, or income of $64: [(100 × $0.08) × 8].

Thus, the formula looks like this:

$$\text{Rate of Return} = \frac{(1660 - 1015) + 64}{1015}$$

which equals

$$\text{Rate of Return} = \frac{645 + 64}{1015} \text{ or } \frac{709}{1015}$$

Divide $709 by $1,015 and you get **69.85%.** And that is your total rate of return.

TO CALCULATE YOUR RATE OF RETURN ON A MUTUAL FUND:

$$\text{Average Total Return} = \frac{(\text{Dividend} + \text{Capital Gains Distributions}) + \dfrac{(\text{Ending NAV} - \text{Beginning NAV})}{\text{Year}}}{\dfrac{(\text{Ending NAV} + \text{Beginning NAV})}{2}}$$

OK, this formula looks substantially more complicated than it really is. Basically, there are three variables you need to know:

1. The beginning NAV, or the net asset value you paid per share, or, if you're calculating the annual return on shares you haven't sold, the NAV at the beginning of the year.

2. The ending NAV, or the net asset value at which you sold each share. Or, for annual-return calculations, the value of the shares at the end of the year.
3. The dividends and capital gains distributions (both long-term and short-term) you received along the way.

So, let's say you bought shares in the WinBig Mutual Fund at $12 each, paying no commission, as is common. Your Beginning NAV is $12.

A year later you sell off all your shares in the fund at $15.43 per share, again paying no commission. Your Ending NAV is $15.43.

Along the way, you received $0.27 per share in dividends and $0.66 per share in capital-gains distributions.

Thus, the formula looks like this:

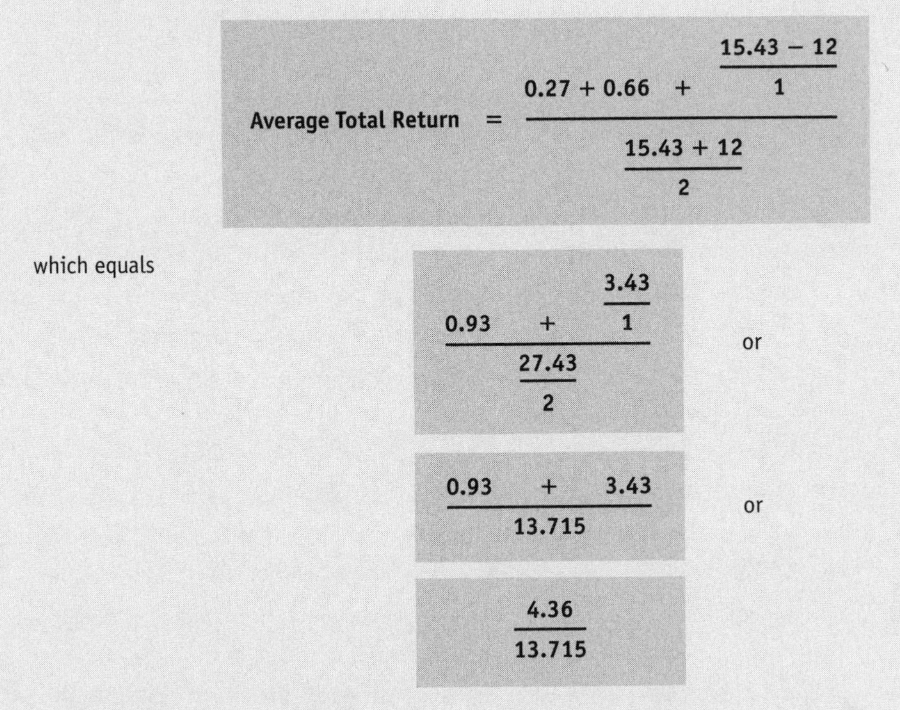

Divide $4.36 by $13.715 and you get **31.8%**, which is your rate of return.

But don't get too hung up on returns; they're only signposts along the way. Whether you beat the market, match the market, or underperform the market with any given investment or in any given year really isn't terribly important. The goal always remains the same: prudent investments that you own for the long haul in a well-diversified portfolio. If you follow that simple rule, your return, whatever it ultimately is, will have served you well in the end.

SIZE MATTERS

Publicly traded companies are ranked by their size: large-cap, mid-cap, small-cap, and micro-cap, where "cap" is short for capitalization, or the cumulative market value of all the company's shares. When Seattle-based banking firm Washington Mutual traded at $42 per share in spring 2005, and had 884.05 million shares outstanding, it had a so-called market capitalization of $37.13 billion (42 × 884.05 million). That's large. Thus, the bank known as WaMu is a large-cap stock.

Professional investors have various definitions of what dollar value defines large, medium, small, and micro. But in general, large-cap represents a company in which the shares are worth a cumulative $5 billion or more; mid-cap is generally between $500 million and $5 billion; small-cap is $50 million to $500 million; and micro-cap is $50 million or less. In general, large-caps grow more slowly because of their size, while micro-caps often grow more rapidly. The trade-off: large-caps tend to be more stable, while micro-caps tend to be as volatile as a can of shaken soda.

Even for mutual-fund investors these distinctions are relevant, since mutual funds are rated and compared against one another based on the category they fit into—and those categories are generally differentiated on the basis of the size of companies the fund owns.

By the way, there are also penny stocks, which don't literally have to sell for pennies a share, though many do. In general, they're stocks priced below $5 a share that have a limited trading history and which don't trade on a major exchange like the New York Stock Exchange or Nasdaq. Many trade on the Pink Sheets (www.pinksheets.com), an electronic bulletin board, not an exchange, where investors essentially post their interest in buying or selling shares of various unlisted stocks. To confuse the matter, not all Pink Sheets stocks are penny stocks; some trade for thousands of dollars a share.

INDEX INVESTING: NO EFFORT REQUIRED

If you want to be an investor, yet you don't want to put any effort into researching stocks or bonds or analyzing what mutual fund is right for you, then here's the answer you're looking for: index funds.

With a single investment you own the Standard & Poor's 500-stock index. Then you can get back to fishing or crocheting or creating the cure for the common cold.

The Fidelity Spartan 500 Index Fund (symbol: FSMKX) and the Vanguard 500 Index Fund (VFINX) are both ultralow-cost index funds that track the S&P 500. Own them and you own the market. Whatever the S&P does over time—and over long periods of time it marches higher—is essentially what you'll do over time.

That's all it takes to be an investor.

EXCHANGE-TRADED FUNDS: MINIMAL EFFORT REQUIRED

One step up from an index fund is an exchange-traded fund, known simply as an ETF.

These are essentially index mutual funds, only they trade like shares of stock. That means that instead of buying an index fund from a mutual-fund company, you buy an ETF on Wall Street, since most ETFs trade on the American Stock Exchange.

ETFs offer some benefits over index funds: First, you have more control over the price. ETFs trade throughout the day, just like shares of stock. Mutual funds are priced once a day, after the market closes, so you never know at what price you're buying and selling until after the fact. With an ETF you can establish the maximum you're willing to pay to buy and the minimum you're willing to accept to sell through what are known as "limit orders." Of course, there's no guarantee the ETF will ever hit your limit.

Also, for so-called buy-and-hold investors, or those who plan to own the investment for a long time, ETF fees are generally smaller than with mutual funds, though that is not universal. For ETFs with lower fees, investors save thousands of dollars over time, meaning you ultimately have a bigger pot of money.

Finally, ETFs offer a broader selection of indexes to choose from, with new ones cropping up all the time. ETFs index everything from the S&P 500 to the Russell 2000 small-cap stock index to the price of gold to a variety of individual countries to the price of a barrel of crude oil.

For armchair investors who want to diversify and build a portfolio of several indexes, ETFs offer the best option.

DOLLAR-COST AVERAGING

If you want to be slightly more active in your investing, and if you're going to buy individual stocks and mutual funds, dollar-cost averaging is a conservative approach to building assets over time. The strength of dollar-cost averaging is that it imposes fiscal prudence and requires that you invest consistently—both of which will serve you well over the long run.

No investor knows if a particular stock or mutual fund will be worth more or less tomorrow than it is today—and anyone who tries to sell you a system to do that is ripping you off. Moreover, if you spent all your time trying to divine that answer you'd be so paralyzed by indecision that you'd never get around to actually investing your money. Dollar-cost averaging takes the guesswork out of investing, since you routinely invest a fixed amount each month in a particular stock or mutual fund, regardless of price, every month or quarter. Over time, you are in most cases lowering the average price at which you buy your investment. The strategy works this way because you buy more shares when the price is lower and fewer shares when the price is higher; over time, then, your average cost per share will typically be less than had you invested your entire sum at once.

Here's how it works: You like a particular company but you're not sure if the stock is going up or down, and you don't want to stick your entire $10,000 nut into the company's shares all at once, since if they fall you'll be able to afford more. Of course, you don't want to miss out on the current price in the event the shares move higher. Caught between going all in or sitting on the sidelines, you opt for a middle ground: You invest $2,500 every quarter for the next year. This is what your purchase record might look like:

Period	Price/Share	Shares Bought	Amount Invested
1st quarter	$25	100	$2,500
2nd quarter	22	113.64	$2,500
3rd quarter	17	147.06	$2,500
4th quarter	24	104.17	$2,500
	Total	464.87	$10,000
	Average price per share		$21.51

Had you invested your $10,000 lump sum to begin with, you would have lost money over the year, since the shares were $1 lower 12 months later. However, through dollar-cost averaging you actually have a profit of $3.49 a share ($25 – $21.51) because the lower-priced purchases along the way reduced your overall per-share cost in the stock.

Dollar-cost averaging works best with companies that allow you to make additional purchases of stock by sending a check in on a monthly or quarterly basis—this is known as a Direct Stock Purchase plan, or DSP. This keeps you from having to pay additional brokerage commissions with every purchase. A Dividend Reinvestment Plan, or DRiP, works similarly in that your dividends are automatically reinvested in the company's shares each quarter.

DirectInvesting.com (www. directinvesting.com) lists the companies that offer DSP and DRiP options. It also provides services to help you enroll electronically in the plans in which you want to participate.

To dollar-cost–average in a mutual fund, you can either send a check to the fund on a regular basis, maybe monthly or quarterly, or you can arrange for the fund to routinely draw a predetermined sum of money from your bank account on a preset schedule. Nearly every fund offers this option.

The one chore with dollar-cost averaging comes at tax time, when you'll need to know your original costs in the stock or mutual fund in order to accurately determine the size of your gains or losses. This exercise can be particularly grinding if you have invested over many years through a DRiP, since the purchase of additional shares with your dividend payment each quarter opens a new transaction that you must track. To help keep up with all this, use the worksheet on the next page. Fill in the data each time you buy a stock or mutual fund using either the dollar-cost averaging method or with a DRiP or DSP:

KEEPING TRACK OF YOUR DOLLAR-COST AVERAGING AND DRiP INVESTMENTS

DOLLAR-COST AVERAGING, DRiPS AND DSPS

(Use these columns to help determine gain/loss)

Date	Amount Invested	Price per Share	Shares Purchased	Sales Price	Gain/(Loss) (sales price – amount invested)

To calculate your average cost per share, plug the appropriate numbers into this formula:

$$\text{Average Cost per Share} = \frac{\text{Total Dollars Invested}}{\text{Total Number of Shares Purchased}}$$

MUTUAL FUNDS

Date	Type of Transaction*	Amount Invested	Share Price	Shares Bought	Cumulative Shares Owned†

* Capital gain distribution; dividend distribution; purchase with additional capital; redemption.

† Add the current number of shares bought to the last entry in Cumulative Shares Owned to keep a running tally of total shares owned.

To calculate your cost basis for any shares you sell, a necessity come tax time, follow this template:

Date of Sale	Original Date of Purchase	Original Transaction	Shares Sold	×	Share Price	=	Proceeds

Proceeds	–	Original Amount Invested	=	Gain/(Loss)

CHAPTER 7

Retirement Planning: Feathering the Nest Egg

For most people, this is what investing is all about: preparing for that day you retire and live the rest of your life off the money you've accumulated.

Getting to that day, of course, is a daunting thought. So expensive it promises to be that it's hard to really fathom the magnitude of money you need to amass. When you earn $30,000 to $50,000 a year, and you realize you might need $1 million or more, you laugh to yourself and say, "Right! And where's the guidebook to successful bank robbery?"

Without question, that will be a challenge. But a challenge is not an impossibility; it's a very real possibility that just takes planning, commitment, and execution. Just remember: If you fail to plan, then you plan to fail—and you will suffer in the end.

Ultimately arriving at the destination you envision starts with what is for most people the most difficult part of the process: determining the finish line.

HOW MUCH WILL I NEED IN RETIREMENT?

This is the finish line—the rough estimate of how much you'll need after you retire to live out the rest of your life in the lifestyle you want.

The estimate is rough because it's basically impossible to know with great certainty exactly what your life will cost in the future. Suffice it to say that retirement is the single largest expense most people will ever save for.

A house is certainly expensive and is often the biggest single purchase people ever make. And college costs can be a tremendous drain on your savings and income. But they are wan candlelight in comparison to the floodlight required to brighten your retirement. Depending upon the style of living you're accustomed to and how long you end up living after you leave work, retirement could easily cost into the millions of dollars when it's all said and done.

But what goal should *you* be saving toward specifically? That's the unknown that stymies so many people. Who knows what life will cost decades from now? Who knows how your income will change through the years? Who knows what level of returns your savings and investments will generate? Who knows what inflation will do?

All of those factors weigh on what you ultimately will have to live on in retirement and how much that retirement will cost. Honestly, trying to plan for that future is a guessing game, because the goal you think you're shooting for could be well short of where you really need to be once you arrive—or it could be well beyond it. Still, preparing for what tomorrow might bring is magnitudes smarter than just winging it on a hope and a prayer that all will work out OK.

So, you probably want to start saving now.

The worksheet on pages 147–152 is designed to give you an idea of how much money you need to accumulate to cover the basics of life, rather than the amount of money you'll need to replace your standard of living. (Visit www.WSJ.com/BookTools for an interactive version of the worksheet.) Many retirement plans start with the idea that you need to replace between 70% and 100% of your income to live in retirement as you do in your working career. That's fine. But there are flaws in that approach. First, the "income" component of such a plan is based on your income just prior to retirement, and guessing at what that will be—and, in turn, what your standard of living will be—is like trying to predict in 2005 the winner of the 2027 World Series. Second, that income-replacement rule-of-thumb presumes you want or expect that same style of living, though some people expect to scale back their life, while others expect to ramp it up substantially.

Basic expenses, however, are, well, basic. They don't change all that much, aside from rising over time because of the effects of inflation, but you can adjust for that in your planning. You're not going to eat more food when you retire.

RETIREMENT PLANNING: WHAT'S IT GOING TO COST?

Funding your retirement is likely to be the most expensive proposition you face. After retiring, you'll need enough money to pay for your life for potentially decades. That promises to be pretty expensive. Many retirement planning guides say you'll need in retirement 70% to 100% of your pre-retirement income to live your life. Maybe. But a more reasoned approach is that you'll need enough in retirement to ensure that you can afford your basic monthly expenses—housing, food, electricity, insurance, property taxes (if any). This worksheet is designed to help you gauge what those costs could be in the future, and from there help you determine how much more you need to save based on how much you already have. Note that this worksheet provides just a ballpark estimate. Retirement has so many moving parts that it is almost impossible to account for all the possible, or even probable, scenarios.

STEP 1: BASIC EXPENSES TODAY . . .

How much does your basic life cost today? The rent or mortgage you pay; the water and sewer; electricity; heating oil; food; various life, auto, health, and home owner's insurance policies. These are the absolute basics of keeping you fed, sheltered, and protected from a financial catastrophe, and most, if not all, of these costs will follow you into retirement. This does not include discretionary expenses such as dinners out, vacations, or season tickets to your favorite sports team. You must determine how much of those costs you'll need to replace in retirement, since some costs might no longer exist, such as a mortgage. Then again, maybe other costs will spring up, like unexpected medical care. Typically, you want to replace no less than 70% of your current basic costs; replacing 100% is more conservative.

Cost of your basic monthly expenses today (Consider using many of the expenses you listed on your **Emergency Expense** worksheet, since most of those, aside from education expenses, represent fixed monthly costs you'll likely face in retirement.)	1
What percentage of those expenses to replace	2
Total basic monthly expenses to replace	3 $
	× 12
Total annual basic expenses, today's dollars:	4 $

STEP 2: . . . AND BASIC INCOME TODAY

Social Security is likely to play some role in your retirement, assuming you're not one of those government workers that isn't part of the system. Every year, the Social Security Administration mails you a Statement of Benefits that shows how much monthly income you're in line to receive at retirement. If you don't have that statement, you can log onto www.socialsecurity.gov and request a copy. Or, you can go to www.ssa.gov/OACT/quickcalc/ and estimate what your benefits will be at retirement.

Insert the monthly value here:	5
	× 12
Annual Social Security income:	6 $

If you're fortunate to have a guaranteed pension coming from an employer, ask your Human Resources department if it can estimate what your monthly check will be at retirement. Ask if the sum is in today's dollars or inflation-adjusted dollars. If it's today's dollars, you'll need to go through the same inflation-adjustment process from above.

Estimated pension income:	7
Total expected income in today's dollars:	8 $
Shortfall:	9 $

STEP 3: THE COSTS OF TOMORROW

The thing about tomorrow is that it's likely to be more expensive than today. That's the impact of inflation. You must adjust for inflation to determine how many future dollars you're likely to need. To do that, you first need to estimate the

(continued)

number of years before you retire, rounding it off to the number in the chart closest to your date. For instance, if you expect to retire in 17 years, choose 18 below.

How many years before you retire: [10]

Next, determine what rate of inflation you expect over time. Historically, inflation has run about 3%. Using the chart below, match the number of years in Box 5 above with your expectations for inflation . . .

. . . and insert that number here: [11]

YEARS BEFORE RETIREMENT	INFLATION RATE								
	1%	1.50%	2%	2.50%	3%	3.50%	4%	4.50%	5%
2	1.0201	1.0302	1.0404	1.0506	1.0609	1.0712	1.0816	1.0920	1.1025
5	1.0510	1.0773	1.1041	1.1314	1.1593	1.1877	1.2167	1.2462	1.2763
7	1.0721	1.1098	1.1487	1.1887	1.2299	1.2723	1.3159	1.3609	1.4071
10	1.1046	1.1605	1.2190	1.2801	1.3439	1.4106	1.4802	1.5530	1.6289
12	1.1268	1.1956	1.2682	1.3449	1.4258	1.5111	1.6010	1.6959	1.7959
15	1.1610	1.2502	1.3459	1.4483	1.5580	1.6753	1.8009	1.9353	2.0789
18	1.1961	1.3073	1.4282	1.5597	1.7024	1.8575	2.0258	2.2085	2.4066
20	1.2202	1.3469	1.4859	1.6386	1.8061	1.9898	2.1911	2.4117	2.6533
22	1.2447	1.3876	1.5460	1.7216	1.9161	2.1315	2.3699	2.6337	2.9253
25	1.2824	1.4509	1.6406	1.8539	2.0938	2.3632	2.6658	3.0054	3.3864
28	1.3213	1.5172	1.7410	1.9965	2.2879	2.6202	2.9987	3.4297	3.9201
30	1.3478	1.5631	1.8114	2.0976	2.4273	2.8068	3.2434	3.7453	4.3219
32	1.3749	1.6103	1.8845	2.2038	2.5751	3.0067	3.5081	4.0900	4.7649
35	1.4166	1.6839	1.9999	2.3732	2.8139	3.3336	3.9461	4.6673	5.5160

Multiply the number in Box 4 by that in Box 6 to determine your

. . . total annual shortfall, inflation adjusted at retirement: [12 $]

STEP 4: WHAT'S IN YOUR NEST EGG . . . AND HOW BIG WILL IT BE?

Since Social Security typically covers roughly 40% of the average retiree's income needs, the money you save in banking and investment accounts will play a significant role in your retirement lifestyle.

Current size of nest egg [13]

Now, you need to account for the growth of your nest egg over time since it will rack up investment returns. On the chart below, locate how many years you have until retirement, and then find where it intersects with a rate of return you think is likely on your money. Historically, the stock market has grown at 10% a year, but most people don't have 100% of the cash in stocks. You need to account for the much slower growth of bonds and cash accounts like CDs and money-market funds. Anywhere from 5% to 8% is a more likely figure.

YEARS BEFORE RETIREMENT	INFLATION RATE								
	3%	4%	5%	6%	7%	8%	9%	10%	11%
2	1.06090	1.08160	1.10250	1.12360	1.14490	1.16640	1.18810	1.21000	1.23210
5	1.15927	1.21665	1.27628	1.33823	1.40255	1.46933	1.53862	1.61051	1.68506
7	1.22987	1.31593	1.40710	1.50363	1.60578	1.71382	1.82804	1.94872	2.07616
10	1.34392	1.48024	1.62889	1.79085	1.96715	2.15892	2.36736	2.59374	2.83942
12	1.42576	1.60103	1.79586	2.01220	2.25219	2.51817	2.81266	3.13843	3.49845
15	1.55797	1.80094	2.07893	2.39656	2.75903	3.17217	3.64248	4.17725	4.78459
18	1.70243	2.02582	2.40662	2.85434	3.37993	3.99602	4.71712	5.55992	6.54355
20	1.80611	2.19112	2.65330	3.20714	3.86968	4.66096	5.60441	6.72750	8.06231
22	1.91610	2.36992	2.92526	3.60354	4.43040	5.43654	6.65860	8.14027	9.93357
25	2.09378	2.66584	3.38635	4.29187	5.42743	6.84848	8.62308	10.83471	13.58546
28	2.28793	2.99870	3.92013	5.11169	6.64884	8.62711	11.16714	14.42099	18.57990
30	2.42726	3.24340	4.32194	5.74349	7.61226	10.06266	13.26768	17.44940	22.89230
32	2.57508	3.50806	4.76494	6.45339	8.71527	11.73708	15.76333	21.11378	28.20560
35	2.81386	3.94609	5.51602	7.68609	10.67658	14.78534	20.41397	28.10244	38.57485

Insert the number from the chart here:	14
Multiply Box 15 by Box 16 for estimated future value of nest egg at retirement:	15 $

STEP 5: HOW MUCH TO SAVE . . .

So, the next logical question: If I have a shortfall, how much do I need to save? You already have part, or possibly all, of that shortfall saved—your current nest egg that, hopefully, will grow over time to resemble the number in Box 15. But this is where retirement planning gets messy. How long your nest egg ultimately lasts depends on a wide number of variables, most outside your control. Investment returns will vary widely from year to year; inflation could rise or fall; your need for cash from one year to next could change and the rate at which your profits are taxed depends greatly on where the money is coming from: The entire value of the withdrawal from a 401(k) or IRA is taxed as ordinary income; the withdrawal from a Roth 401(k) or Roth IRA is untaxed. Profits from stocks are taxed at capital gains rates; profits on the sale of bonds are taxed at higher ordinary income rates. All of these variables determine how many years your nest egg will last.

And that's the problem: that all of those variables are largely unknowable, as is the biggest variable of all—how many years you'll live in retirement. You don't know if you'll live 40 years or four months, and longevity plays a huge role, since the longer you live, the more money you'll need to fund your life. Statistically, people who reach retirement will live for another 18 to 20 years, though increasing numbers of retirees are living for 30 years or longer.

To get an idea of how these variables flow through your nest egg, take a look at this chart. It shows how a $1 million nest egg at the beginning of your retirement changes over time based upon annual withdrawals and the growth and taxation of the portfolio.

Let's start in Year 1, the year you retire.

Beginning Value is the number in Box 15—the amount of money you begin with in retirement. In this case, let's assume it's $1 million.

Annual Withdrawal represents the amount of money you draw out of your nest egg at the beginning of the year for the expenses beyond what your inflation-adjusted Social Security/pension income will cover. This is the number in Box 12. In this example, we'll assume the number of $60,000 to begin with, and we'll assume the withdrawals rise 3% a year. To calculate the value for each of the remaining years, multiply the previous year's value by 1.03, so that $60,000 in Year 1 is $61,800 in Year 2.

Investable Assets is the remaining amount of money that can generate returns for the year. This is the Beginning Value minus the Annual Withdrawal.

Asset Growth is the return generated by the Investable Assets. You can choose whatever rate of return you deem appropriate. Historically, stocks have grown at roughly 10% a year, though a balanced portfolio of stocks, bonds, and cash is more likely to grow over time at between 5% and 7% a year. Keep in mind that investment returns do not move in average annual fashion, meaning they don't routinely go up 7% a year in a straight line. Some years are up, some are down, and what string of returns you see during retirement will play a very large role in how long your nest lasts and how much money you can ultimately withdraw each year. Accumulate a string of bad years just as you retire, and your nest egg may not stretch as far as you hope. This example assumes static growth of 5%. The calculation: Investable Assets multiplied by .05.

Taxes on Growth assumes you pay federal, state, and local taxes at some rate on the asset growth. This is a guess, since your assets will come out of different accounts taxed at different rates. For lower income tax brackets, choose 15%; for middle-income tax brackets choose 25%; for higher income tax brackets choose 35%. And just to show how truly complicated it can be trying to estimate how long your nest egg will last, you also will be taxed on some portion of your annual withdrawal each year if any of that money comes out of a 401(k)/403(b)-type retirement account, a traditional or rollover IRA, or an annuity. For the sake of simplicity, the example below taxes only the asset growth at 25%. The calculation: Asset Growth multiplied by .25.

(continued)

Ending Value is Investable Assets plus Assets Growth minus Taxes on Growth. It is the value of your account at the end of the year, and, thus, the Beginning Value for the next year.

Year	Beginning Value	Annual Withdrawal	Investable Assets	Asset Growth	Taxes on Growth	Ending Value
1	$1,000,000	−$60,000	$940,000	$47,000	−$11,750	$975,250
2	$ 975,250	−$61,800	$913,450	$27,404	−$ 6,851	$934,003
3	$ 934,003	−$63,654	$870,349	$26,110	−$ 6,528	$889,931
4	$ 889,931	−$65,564	$824,368	$24,731	−$ 6,183	$842,916
5	$ 842,916	−$67,531	$775,386	$23,262	−$ 5,815	$792,832
6	$ 792,832	−$69,556	$723,275	$21,698	−$ 5,425	$739,549
7	$ 739,549	−$71,643	$667,906	$20,037	−$ 5,009	$682,934
8	$ 682,934	−$73,792	$609,141	$18,274	−$ 4,569	$622,847
9	$ 622,847	−$76,006	$546,841	$16,405	−$ 4,101	$559,145
10	$ 559,145	−$78,286	$480,858	$14,426	−$ 3,606	$491,678
11	$ 491,678	−$80,635	$411,043	$12,331	−$ 3,083	$420,291
12	$ 420,291	−$83,054	$337,237	$10,117	−$ 2,529	$344,825
13	$ 344,825	−$85,546	$259,279	$ 7,778	−$ 1,945	$265,113
14	$ 265,113	−$88,112	$177,001	$ 5,310	−$ 1,328	$180,984
15	$ 180,984	−$90,755	$ 90,228	$ 2,707	−$ 677	$ 92,258

Fill in this worksheet based upon your own assumptions to get a feel for the impacts of withdrawals, asset growth, and taxation on your nest egg through the years. This worksheet goes through 20 years; if you want to project out further, follow the same format on a piece of paper. Or, create a spreadsheet on your computer that will allow you to instantly change any and all variables.

Year	Beginning Value	Annual Withdrawal	Investable Assets	Asset Growth	Taxes on Growth	Ending Value
1						
2						
3						
4						
5						
6						
7						
8						
9						
10						
11						
12						
13						
14						
15						
16						
17						
18						
19						
20						

Now that you have an idea of how inexact retirement planning can be, you still have to do something to prepare for the costs you'll face. Since it is tough to know how all the variables will interact in your life years or decades from now, the best you can aim for is to accumulate a sum of money close to the amount you'll need to pay for the basic expenses not covered by your Social Security or pension income—essentially the number in Box 12. But remember: That number in Box 12 is the gap that exists in Year 1 only. You'll need to determine your cumulative gap over the number of years you expect to live in retirement.

The rationale behind this approach: If you save prior to retiring what you're likely to ultimately need throughout retirement to pay the difference between your income and basic expenses, then you should be well covered. Your investments, despite the ups and downs they'll be subjected to, should be large enough to afford your basic expenses—and likely a few perks to make retirement fun. There is a flaw, though: You're likely oversaving with this approach, because it does not take into account how withdrawals, asset growth, and taxation will impact your nest egg specifically. Nevertheless, with this approach you're creating a margin of safety, a buffer to see you through unexpectedly higher costs in retirement—such as for healthcare—or unexpectedly lower or negative returns over consecutive years in your investment portfolio.

You first need to determine your cumulative costs for basic expenses in retirement. To do so you need to estimate

how many years you expect to live in retirement: | 16 |

In the chart below, find where the number of years before you expect to live in retirement intersects with the inflation rate you expect in retirement. Then, multiply that number by the number in Box 12. This represents your

cumulative costs in retirement: | 17 $ |

YEARS IN RETIREMENT	INFLATION RATE								
	1%	1.50%	2%	2.50%	3%	3.50%	4%	4.50%	5%
2	2.0100	2.0150	2.0200	2.0250	2.0300	2.0350	2.0400	2.0450	2.0500
5	5.1010	5.1523	5.2040	5.2563	5.3091	5.3625	5.4163	5.4707	5.5256
7	7.2135	7.3230	7.4343	7.5474	7.6625	7.7794	7.8983	8.0192	8.1420
10	10.4622	10.7027	10.9497	11.2034	11.4639	11.7314	12.0061	12.2882	12.5779
12	12.6825	13.0412	13.4121	13.7956	14.1920	14.6020	15.0258	15.4640	15.9171
15	16.0969	16.6821	17.2934	17.9319	18.5989	19.2957	20.0236	20.7841	21.5786
18	19.6147	20.4894	21.4123	22.3863	23.4144	24.4997	25.6454	26.8551	28.1324
20	22.0190	23.1237	24.2974	25.5447	26.8704	28.2797	29.7781	31.3714	33.0660
22	24.4716	25.8376	27.2990	28.8629	30.5368	32.3289	34.2480	36.3034	38.5052
25	28.2432	30.0630	32.0303	34.1578	36.4593	38.9499	41.6459	44.5652	47.7271
28	32.1291	34.4815	37.0512	39.8598	42.9309	46.2906	49.9676	53.9933	58.4026
30	34.7849	37.5387	40.5681	43.9027	47.5754	51.6227	56.0849	61.0071	66.4388
32	37.4941	40.6883	44.2270	48.1503	52.5028	57.3345	62.7015	68.6662	75.2988
35	41.6603	45.5921	49.9945	54.9282	60.4621	66.6740	73.6522	81.4966	90.3203

Subtract Box 17 from Box 15. This is the gap between your cumulative expenses and the projected value of your nest egg at retirement—essentially the additional amount of money your nest egg must cover: | 18 $ |

You need to examine Box 18 to understand what it means:

If Box 18 is a positive number, meaning the value of your expected nest egg (Box 15) is larger than your expected cumulative costs in retirement (Box 17), then your nest egg ultimately will reach a size large enough to cover your basic expenses in retirement. However, if Box 18 is negative, then the number represents the shortfall that you must save toward.

If Box 18 is negative, divide the amount by 1,000 | 19 $ |

(continued)

In the chart below, locate the number of years you have before retirement (this should be the same number as in Box 10) and find where that intersects the annual rate of return you expect to earn on your investments prior to retiring.

Insert that number here: 20

YEARS BEFORE RETIREMENT	ANNUAL RATE OF RETURN								
	3%	4%	5%	6%	7%	8%	9%	10%	11%
2	40.4812	40.0916	39.7047	39.3206	38.9392	38.5606	38.1847	37.8116	37.4412
5	15.4687	15.0832	14.7046	14.3328	13.9679	13.6097	13.2584	12.9137	12.5758
7	10.7133	10.3355	9.9672	9.6086	9.2593	8.9195	8.5891	8.2679	7.9558
10	7.1561	6.7912	6.4399	6.1021	5.7775	5.4661	5.1676	4.8817	4.6083
12	5.7779	5.4220	5.0822	4.7585	4.4505	4.1579	3.8803	3.6174	3.3689
15	4.4058	4.0635	3.7413	3.4386	3.1549	2.8899	2.6427	2.4127	2.1993
18	3.4972	3.1686	2.8637	2.5816	2.3217	2.0830	1.8644	1.6651	1.4838
20	3.0460	2.7265	2.4329	2.1643	1.9197	1.6977	1.4973	1.3169	1.1552
22	2.6790	2.3685	2.0861	1.8307	1.6009	1.3951	1.2117	1.0491	0.9056
25	2.2421	1.9450	1.6792	1.4430	1.2345	1.0515	0.8920	0.7537	0.6345
28	1.9027	1.6188	1.3691	1.1512	0.9628	0.8009	0.6630	0.5463	0.4481
30	1.7160	1.4408	1.2015	0.9955	0.8197	0.6710	0.5462	0.4424	0.3566
32	1.5542	1.2875	1.0584	0.8638	0.7001	0.5637	0.4512	0.3591	0.2843
35	1.3485	1.0944	0.8802	0.7019	0.5552	0.4359	0.3399	0.2634	0.2029

Finally, multiply Box 19 by Box 20.
This is the amount of money to save monthly to reach your goal: 21 $

One last note: The monthly amount shown in Box 21 might seem outrageous, but remember that it's a function of your expected basic costs in retirement. You might want to revisit those costs to determine if the amount you wrote down in Box 1 accurately captures just your basic monthly expenses. You might be including costs—such as a mortgage—that you may not have in retirement.

You're not going to consume sharply more kilowatt hours of electricity. Your housing costs, assuming you haven't paid off your mortgage, will be in the same ballpark they were two decades earlier—and if your house is paid off, then you can still budget that amount into your planning to cover unexpectedly higher medical or pharmaceutical costs, or whatever. The point is that if you aim to cover your basics, you'll not have to worry about keeping the lights on when you're old or having to skimp on food because your monthly income is too small. And once you know what you need to save to afford your basic needs, you can choose how much to save above that in order to afford whatever realistic retirement lifestyle you envision.

Once you have a goal to shoot toward, you're ready to start fashioning the portfolio you'll need to get you there.

ASSET ALLOCATION: ROCKET SCIENCE FOR BEGINNERS

This is the point where lots of folks give up on investing because they figure that trying to determine what to invest in and how to choose from among thousands upon thousands of stocks, bonds, and mutual funds is just too daunting.

Yet asset allocation is a simple concept: Different types of assets move in different ways, and to be properly diversified you want a mix of those different types of assets so that when one asset is moving down, another is moving up. Stocks, for instance, generally move based on corporate earnings and the outlook for the general economy; bonds generally move with interest rates; gold moves on geopolitical tensions and currency woes; oil moves on waxing and waning fears of supply shortages and the ebb and flow of global energy demands.

NOTE: Studies have shown that more than 90% of a portfolio's overall long-term success depends not on what you own but on how you allocate your money. That means your mix of assets—the assortment of stocks, bonds, cash, real estate, etc., that you own—is more vital than the individual investments themselves.

Investors who owned nothing but stocks when the bear market growled to life in 2000 suffered mightily. But those who mixed in an appropriate dose of bonds never fretted because bonds performed admirably during that period.

For individual investors, asset allocation is no more complex than following your basic tiramisù recipe—it seems challenging and time-consuming if you've never done it, but once you start folding together the marscapone and meringue, you realize it's not so difficult after all, and it doesn't take much time.

The basic rule is this: The younger you are, the more money you should allocate to stocks. The older you grow, the more you increase your exposure to bonds.

The rationale: Younger workers need in their earlier years the growth that stocks provide, while older savers need the safety of high-grade corporate and government bonds to preserve their nest egg before they retire. If the stock market tanks when you're younger, the losses might hurt, but you still have many years—decades, actually—to recoup your mistakes and rebuild your account. Investing too much in bonds early on, however, means you risk not earning enough of a return through the years to accumulate an adequately sized retirement account.

Conversely, if you're older and nearing retirement when the stock market tanks, you won't have nearly enough time to replenish what was lost. That will ultimately crimp your lifestyle in retirement. Putting increasing amounts of your portfolio into bonds as you age protects you from just such a disaster, since the price of high-quality federal, municipal, and corporate bonds don't fall that far, even in a rotten year. Still, you need some money in stocks because the returns that stocks generate over time will help your portfolio keep ahead of inflation. Otherwise, you risk that inflation erodes the value of your nest egg.

ASSET ALLOCATION MODELS

The most generic way to invest your money is the so-called 60-40 split, in which 60% of your dollars go into the stock market while 40% goes into the bond market. That middle-of-the-road allocation provides for growth (via stocks), yet also provides a buffer against volatility while providing consistent income (via bonds). This is one of those you-won't-lose-sleep-at-night portfolios—because while you won't generate gunslinger-like returns of an aggressive investor, you also won't see 90% of the value of your portfolio disappear when those same aggressive stocks flame out.

The stock component is often invested in an S&P 500 index fund, such as the ones offered by Fidelity and Vanguard, both of which are ultralow-cost. The bond component, meanwhile, is typically in U.S. Treasury bonds, the safest bond investment in the world, given that the money is backed by the full faith and credit of the U.S. government. Some investors use municipal bonds or high-grade corporate bonds, both of which can provide slightly beefier returns though with marginally more risk.

NOTE: High-grade corporate bonds are those rated **BBB** and above by Standard & Poor's, or **Baa** and higher by Moody's Investors Service. These ratings are given to companies with the lowest risk of defaulting on their obligation to repay investors like you.

For a slightly more personalized approach, a widely used rule of thumb suggests you subtract your age from 100—or even 120, if you're willing to be more aggressive—and stick that percentage of your portfolio in stocks. The remainder goes into bonds. So, if you happen to be, say, 39 years old, then you'd want either 61% or 81% of your money in stocks, depending on your tolerance for the ups and downs you will invariably experience in the stock market.

This approach is much more sensitive to your working career, since it assures that as you age you automatically scale back your stock exposure and increase

BONDS VERSUS BOND FUNDS

Owning a bond is not the same as owning a bond fund. A bond fund carries greater risks.

When you hold a bond to maturity, you're guaranteed to get back your principal, assuming the bond doesn't default (and default rates are negligible among high-quality corporate bonds and the vast majority of municipal bonds, and U.S. Treasurys never default). While a bond's price will go up and down over time, you will ultimately get back your principal.

That's not necessarily true with a bond fund. A bond fund owns numerous bonds, and portfolio managers continually buy and sell bonds in the fund. Thus, the fund has no set maturity date since the bonds aren't being held to maturity in many cases.

This has the biggest negative effect on investors amid rising interest rates. When rates rise, the value of an existing bond falls. That's because investors would rather own a new bond paying a bigger interest rate than an older bond paying a lower rate. So, the older bond's price falls. Investors who own bonds directly can hold the bond until maturity and never be hurt by the shrunken price, whereas bond-fund investors have no maturity date to look forward to. Thus, bond-fund investors have no guarantee of recouping their original investment at some specific point in time.

AGE-BASED ASSET ALLOCATION RULE OF THUMB

% in Stocks = 100 – Current Age

__________ = 100 – __________

your bond holdings. Plus, it always keeps you in stocks to some degree—well, unless you live past 120.

Retaining some stock-market exposure is important. Stocks provide the fuel a portfolio needs to keep your money growing. After all, you don't know if you'll have four years in retirement or forty, and you don't want your cash to expire before you do.

These rules sound pretty simplistic for the highfalutin world of investing. But they work, and for a very simple reason: You are diversifying your investments and that doesn't require anything more complicated than putting a little bit here and little bit there, and understanding why you're doing so.

WHERE DO I INVEST?

Ok, so you've determined how to split your money between stocks and bonds. Now what?

Well, if you're investing in a 401(k) plan, that's all going to depend on what options you have available, since each plan is different from the next in terms of the investment choices offered. If you're investing in an IRA or in a standard brokerage account, you basically have the entire world of investment options open to you. Either way, unless you want to delve into the nitty-gritty of individual stock selection, you'll probably want to stick with mutual funds, since you're getting professional management and instant diversification at far cheaper prices than you'd pay to do it on your own. So while this is ostensibly about picking funds within the framework of a 401(k), the same principles apply to any other investment account.

Likely your plan offers several stock and bond funds and, probably, some specialty funds. And if it's anything like the typical 401(k) plan, you can choose between twelve and seventeen different options, including a company-stock fund if you work for a publicly traded firm, but more on that in a moment. That should be plenty enough choices to allocate your assets properly and build a portfolio that suits your needs.

STEP 1

Get a list of all the funds your plan offers. You'll find this information in your human resources department or, possibly, online if your company provides Web-based access to your 401(k) account.

STEP 2

Visit www.morningstar.com to research the funds to which you have access in your plan. Here's what you're looking for:

- Funds that have a long history of success within their peer group. This means at least a five-year track record of regularly outperforming the "category" and the "index" against which a particular fund benchmarks its returns. One- and three-year records are too short and don't typically capture changing economic cycles. "Category" designates what type of companies a particular fund owns, such as large-cap value or small-cap growth. You'll find the performance information at Morningstar (www.morningstar.com) under the "Total Returns" tab for each individual fund.
- Funds with low expenses. Fees are the internal costs of running the fund, and span a wide range based upon the category in which a fund invests. Again, Morningstar.com will detail the fees a fund charges (under the "Fees and Expenses" tab) and shows how that fee compares to the category average. The higher the fees, the more money you're paying to own the fund, and the smaller your nest egg is in return. And even though the difference in fees can seem minimal—like, say, 1%—that money compounds and adds up to real dollars over many years.
- Funds that stick to their knitting. If you invest in a small-cap growth fund, you don't want to find that it has migrated over time into large-cap value stocks. The reason: You likely already have a large-cap value fund and you don't want to end up with a portfolio overloaded in one area because of a fund that doesn't stick to what it claims to be doing. Morningstar's "Snapshot" page shows the fund's stated mission in the "key stats" section, while just below, the "portfolio analysis" determines what style the fund is pursuing at the moment, based on the makeup of its investments. You want to see that these two generally match to ensure that you're investing in the type and size of companies that meets your risk-tolerance and asset-allocation needs.
- Funds for which the manager on duty is the manager responsible for the track record. Mutual-fund portfolio managers change fairly frequently, and a fund can often lose whatever mojo it had when a new manager starts reconfiguring the portfolio and basing buy and sell decisions on a different view of the market. The "Management" tab at Morningstar reports when the current manager's tenure began, allowing you to look at the fund's track record over that time. Look for manager consistency.

Put into a single sentence, when it comes to picking mutual funds you want funds that routinely beat their peers or index, which charge fees below the category average, which stick to their stated style, and where the manager you're investing with is the one responsible for the returns.

To put all of this into practice means you ultimately have to make investment decisions on your own. If you're the type who wants to get your hands into the mix and research mutual funds yourself, you can find a variety of information at Yahoo! Finance and particularly at Morningstar.

If that sort of research sounds as fun as dental surgery without the anesthesia, here's a cheat sheet to help:

- If you have access to an S&P 500 Index fund, that's where you want to stick the largest portion of your stock-market allocation. All 401(k) plans generally have one of these. If you own no other stock-market exposure, a fund that shadows the S&P 500 will serve you well over time, since over the long-term the U.S. stock market trends upward because of the ever-growing economy. Plus, the internal fees with index funds are some of the lowest in the mutual-fund world. If your plan does not offer an S&P 500 fund or some similar broad-market fund, then go with the best large-company stock fund among the selections you have—with "best" being determined by your research from above.

- Put a small percentage in small-company stocks. Historically, this has been a top-performing fund class over long periods. But you don't want to overdo it: small-company stocks are very aggressive and risky, since small companies not only grow fast, they implode fast. You might find in your 401(k) plan a small-cap index fund that tracks the Russell 2000; that's the best bet. If not, you'll probably have a single, actively managed small-cap fund as your only choice. Beggars can't be choosers.

- Venture abroad. Most 401(k) plans offer an international fund of some sort. Put a small portion (no more than 20%) of your stock-market allocation into international stocks. They are risky, no doubt. They are volatile. But they actually improve the overall stability of your portfolio and enhance the returns. That's because the U.S. is rarely the best-performing market in the world; in any given year, any of numerous other markets around the globe claim that distinction. Plus, owning just American companies limits your growth prospects, since the world is filled with very good, very profitable companies that do not trade on the New York Stock Exchange. Some 401(k) plans will offer any of a variety of international index funds, some will offer actively managed funds. In this instance, actively managed funds are often better. International index funds typically own the biggest companies in a particular country; that's fine, but many of those companies have economic ties in some fashion to the U.S. marketplace. Good international-fund managers are better at looking past the obvious, large companies and finding the solid, smaller local companies responsible for much of a country's underlying growth, and which aren't tied to U.S. consumers in any real way.

- Buy some real estate. Not the kind your house sits on, mind you, but rather an index fund built of real estate investment trusts, or REITs. Not all 401(k) plans offer such an option, though the numbers are increasing. Statistically, real estate provides a counterbalance in a portfolio since it has very little correlation to the movements of the stock and bond markets. That means real estate largely moves independently of stocks and bonds, providing added diversification to a portfolio. All you need is 5% of your overall portfolio in REIT shares and you're fine.

- Own an intermediate-term bond index fund, if your plan offers one. This is a fund that owns bonds with maturities of between four and ten years; such a fund is often in the sweet spot of the bond market. If your plan doesn't offer a bond-index fund, then go with the bond fund that has an "average duration" in the five-to-seven-year range, or something close to that. You can find that average duration number in the fund's prospectus, though going to Morningstar, plugging in the fund's five-letter ticker symbol, and reading about the details on the "Snapshot" page is far easier.

- Go with a TIPS fund if you have access to one. TIPS stands for Treasury Inflation-Protected Securities, U.S. government securities designed to provide a return that always beats inflation. You can't go wrong staying ahead of inflation, since it means your dollars are growing faster than the price of bread at the corner market.

- Skip sector funds. Individual investors often gravitate to funds that specialize in one corner of the Wall Street market, particularly technology, hoping to score a big return. They often wind up getting burned instead, because sector funds tend to be more volatile and aggressive—basically, risky—than are plain-vanilla, broad-based mutual funds. There's no reason to gamble with your future simply to try to squeeze a marginal bit of additional return from your portfolio by taking on substantially more risk.

- Finally, if you don't want the hassle of trying to figure out any of this, stick your entire 401(k) balance in a lifecycle fund, a mutual fund built to be a one-stop shop for investors who don't want to have to think about owning anything other than a single investment. Lifecycle funds have targeted maturity dates as much as thirty or forty years into the future. As such, they change with you as you age, growing increasingly risk-averse as you grow older and the targeted maturity date draws nearer. Equally important: You aren't likely to rack up big losses since the funds are diversified across different types of investments. These funds are growing increasingly popular in retirement plans, because with one investment decision you're adequately diversified and properly allocated instantly based on your age—now and in the future.

WHAT MIGHT A DIVERSIFIED PORTFOLIO LOOK LIKE?

This is where all your research and calculations come together: You have to figure out what to invest in. Pulling that trigger can be the most terrifying part of the process since no one wants to make a bad decisions and possibly lose money.

To get an idea of what kinds of mutual funds you might look for, examine the chart on the next page. These selections are based on Morningstar data from mid-2005, and are not recommendations but simply an illustration of how to design various types of portfolios, based upon the asset-allocation model that you determine best fits your needs. Inside a 401(k) you aren't likely to find all of those funds (though you'll have access to them if your 401(k) plan offers a so-called brokerage window that lets you transact in a brokerage account). Still, you're likely to have similar funds in your plan.

If you invest in any of the various types of IRAs, you'll have access to these funds, as well as thousands more. You're goal isn't to necessarily mimic the funds listed here, since performance can lag and managers change and funds lose their focus—though that's probably not going to happen to any real degree with the index funds. The goal, instead, is to mimic the overall theme of the individual portfolios shown.

SAMPLE ASSET ALLOCATION MODELS

TRADITIONAL 60-40 SPLIT

Stock Component (60%)	
Vanguard 500 Index (VFINX)	45%
Vanguard Total International Stock Index (VGTSX)	
or	
Fidelity Spartan International Index (FSIIX)	10%
Vanguard REIT Index (VGSIX)	5%
Bond Component (40%)	
Pimco Total Return C (PTTCX)	30%
Vanguard Inflation-Protected Securities (VIPSX)	10%
Total	100%

CONSERVATIVE 25-75 SPLIT

Stock Component (25%)	
Vanguard 500 Index (VFINX)	20%
Vanguard Total International Stock Index (VGTSX)	
or	
Fidelity Spartan International Index (FSIIX)	2.5%
Vanguard REIT Index (VGSIX)	2.5%
Bond Component (75%)	
Pimco Total Return C (PTTCX)	60%
Vanguard Inflation-Protected Securities (VIPSX)	15%
Total	100%

AGGRESSIVE 85-15 SPLIT

Stock Component (85%)	
Mairs & Power Growth (MPGFX)	50%
Bridgeway Ultra-Small Co. Market (BRSIX)	10%
Dodge & Cox International Stock (DODFX)	20%
Matthews Pacific Tiger (MAPTX)	5%
Bond Component (15%)	
Pimco Total Return C (PTTCX)	10%
Northeast Investors (NTHEX)	5%
Total	100%

Note: These selections are as of August 2005. Selections can change over time with performance.

COMPANY STOCK: BUY, SELL, OR HOLD?

You might think your employer is the best in the world. You might think that because you work there you have a good feel for the company's stability, its future prospects, and its ability to continue as a successful, ongoing firm. You might think that because you know all of this from an insider's perspective, then it makes sense for you to load up on company stock in your retirement plan, or to buy as much of it as you can through payroll deduction in an employee stock purchase plan.

Right. And workers at Enron Corporation felt the exact same level of confidence in the months before that Houston energy concern imploded in one of the biggest financial fraud and accounting scandals on record. At the time, Enron was part of the Standard & Poor's 500-stock index; its company debt was highly rated by all the ratings agencies. In short, Enron, on the surface, was a model corporate citizen—that ultimately robbed many of its workers of their retirement when, after the financial shenanigans began to unravel, the value of the stock plunged to pennies a share from in excess of $90.

The point is this: Do not invest too much in company stock. From a prudent investor's viewpoint, you are taking on excessive single-company risk. Even if the shares don't implode as Enron's did, you still face the potential for financial heartbreak if the price of your employer's shares, like those of, say, drug giant Schering-Plough, falls from $60 into the low teens on weak corporate performance.

What defines "too much" company stock depends on your tolerance for the inherent risks. But by most standards of prudence, no more than about 10% of your overall portfolio should be invested in a single stock—and that includes your employer's stock.

THE ABCs OF IRAs

IRAs, or individual retirement accounts, are tax-advantaged retirement savings accounts. The money you invest comes from dollars that have already been taxed, so unlike with a 401(k) contribution you get no immediate tax benefit. However, the earnings grow either tax-deferred or tax-free, depending on the type of IRA you own and, again depending on which IRA you own, you may be eligible to deduct all or a portion of your contribution on your annual tax return.

That seems simple enough. The challenges arise from the fact that there are several different types of IRAs, and each has different limits and restrictions and eligibility rules that can make investing in an IRA mind-numbingly complex at times. Indeed, the rules governing traditional IRAs alone can seem as clear as the technical explanations for programming a VCR. Here's a graphical representation of IRS Publication 590, which details who can deduct their annual IRA contributions on tax returns. This is for the 2004 tax year; the income limits increase over time.

Modified Adjusted Gross Income ($)	Single		Married, filing jointly			
			Spouse participates in employer's plan		Spouse doesn't participate in employer's plan	
	You participate in employer's plan	You don't participate in employer's plan	You participate in employer's plan	You don't participate in employer's plan	You participate in employer's plan	You don't participate in employer's plan
Below 45,000	Full	Full	Full	Full	Full	Full
45,000 to 54,999	Partial	Full	Full	Full	Full	Full
55,000 to 64,999	None	Full	Full	Full	Full	Full
65,000 to 74,999	None	Full	Partial	Full	Partial	Full
75,000 to 150,000	None	Full	None	Full	None	Full
150,001 to 159,999	None	Full	None	Partial	None	Full
Above 160,000	None	Full	None	None	None	Full

Unlike a 401(k) plan you might have access to at work and which generally offers a limited selection of investments, IRAs allow you to buy just about any sort of investment you come across, including several nontraditional assets such as precious metals and real estate—though for most investors, mutual funds are usually the best bet since they don't require nearly the same degree of attention that some other investments demand.

As with most tax-advantaged retirement savings plans, if you dip into your IRA before you retire or before you're fifty-nine and a half, you'll pay taxes at ordinary-income rates on both the original contributions and any earnings, plus you're hit with a penalty equal to 10% of the amount of money you withdraw. Under certain situations, the IRS allows you to withdraw IRA money early without penalty. Those reasons, though, are very narrow, including distributions made because of your total and permanent disability; distributions made to an ex-spouse as part of a legal order; distributions made to pay for medical insurance for yourself, your spouse, and your dependents, but only if certain conditions apply; distributions of $10,000 or less made for the first-time purchase of a home; distributions made for qualified educational expenses.

Once you pass fifty-nine and a half, withdrawals from an IRA are taxed at whatever your ordinary income tax rate is at the time without penalty. And once you hit seventy and a half you face mandatory withdrawal, what's known as an annual "required minimum distribution." Fail to do that, and you face a steep penalty: 50% of the amount of money you should have withdrawn. (The rules differ with a Roth IRA, where you have no required distribution; of course, you also don't get to deduct your contribution each year.)

The question you must ask yourself: Which IRA is right for me?

The chart on page 163 will help you determine that, based on where the money is coming from that you want to contribute and other retirement savings accounts that you might be contributing to already.

ANNUITIES: GREAT FOR SOME; LOUSY FOR MANY

Though annuities are investments, they're also a form of insurance—insurance that most people don't understand and don't use properly.

Too many buyers stuff money into an annuity like they would a bank certificate of deposit: they invest, then reclaim their money in a lump sum a few years later. You can do that, sure, but that's like buying a new sports car just to drive two blocks once a week to the corner grocer; you're not really tapping into what the purchase has to offer.

With an annuity, that means you're skipping out on the very reason annuities exist: a guaranteed base of income. In retirement, that guarantee can mean a lot, particularly since the income can be structured to last for as long as you live—no matter how long that ultimately is. Such an arrangement can relieve a

WHICH IRA IS BEST FOR ME?

	Deductible	Nondeductible	Roth	SEP
PROS	During saving phase, contributions are tax deductible, up to a certain limit—$4,000 in 2006, and that rises over time. Contributions and earnings grow tax-deferred. Can withdraw funds early, without penalty, *for certain narrowly defined needs.* At age 50 or above, can save an additional amount as part of the "catch-up" provisions.	Contributions and earnings grow tax-deferred. Contributions can be reclaimed without taxes or penalties. Anyone can contribute, even if you have other retirement savings accounts, so long as you have earned income. At age 50 or above, can save an additional amount as part of the "catch-up" provisions.	Earnings grow tax-free, meaning you can ultimately withdraw contributions and all earnings without paying taxes. You can withdraw total amount of all contributions, tax and penalty free, at any time. No required minimum distributions at any age. At age 50 or above, can save an additional amount as part of the "catch-up" provisions.	Potentially larger contribution limit—up to 20% of your net self-employment income, or a maximum of $42,000 in 2005. Contributions come from your business, as well as any income you draw from the business. As such, contributions lower the taxes on your reportable business income, as well as taxes on your personal income.
CONS	Earnings are taxed as ordinary income at withdrawal. At certain income levels, your ability to contribute phases out. If you already contribute to a company-sponsored retirement plan, you're often ineligible. If you withdraw the money early, generally before 59½, you pay taxes plus a 10% penalty. Must take required minimum distributions by age 70½.	Contributions are not tax-deductible. Requires an extra layer of paperwork; if you forget to file it, the IRS fines you and you might ultimately owe taxes on the money at withdrawal, even though you already paid taxes on that money to begin with. Can only contribute up to level of your earned income if that income is less than the maximum IRA contribution.	Contributions are not tax-deductible. At certain income levels—the same as with a deductible IRA—your ability to contribute phases out.	Must have self-employment income; if not, you can't contribute.
WHO IT'S RIGHT FOR	Just about anyone who doesn't already contribute to a company-sponsored retirement savings plan.	Very few people, actually. This is known as the IRA-of-last-resort since it has no really compelling tax advantages.	If you expect to be in the same or higher tax bracket in retirement than you are in while contributing, the Roth is a good choice, since you will ultimately accumulate more money than with a deductible IRA, which will be taxed at higher, ordinary-income levels.	Excellent option for self-employed workers or those who earn extra income doing freelance or consulting work, since the larger contribution limits allow for significantly larger savings.

NUMBERS LIE

Plug this calculation into any financial program: $100 invested on the first of every month for 30 years at an average annual return of 10%.

The answer you'll get is $227,932.53.

Mathematically, that's true. But don't believe it.

The chances you actually reach that level depend on any number of variables, including the direction of the stock and bond market, the impact of inflation on the markets, and the sequence of returns you get in the market from one year to the next.

In short, when it comes to planning, you need to know that this sort of A + B = C analysis is simplistic and can dish up an unwarranted sense of security since, in most cases, the end result overshoots the amount you'll likely have.

The reason: Aside from fixed-rate assets such as savings accounts, CDs, and bonds held to maturity, investment returns do not move in "average-annual" steps. Stocks historically have returned about 10% a year, but those returns have never been in a straight line. Some years are up 1%, some are down 20%. You may never experience an actual 10% return in your portfolio. The fact is, you have no idea what range of returns you'll get and in what sequence you'll get them.

So, never accept from a financial advisor—or a computer financial-planning program—any calculation that projects a future portfolio value based on an average-annual-return model.

A more useful barometer is a future value determined through Monte Carlo analysis—a mathematical model that grew out of the Manhattan Project that built the atomic bomb in the 1940s. Named for the European casino capital, Monte Carlo describes, much like a weather report, the probability of achieving some result based on dozens, hundreds, or even thousands of variables, all mixing in random fashion. Monte Carlo models run hundreds or thousands or millions of iterations, each time randomly dipping into a preassigned pool of possible variables, then plotting the results. Ultimately, a bell-shaped curve results, with the most likely outcomes clustering near the bell's dome, and increasingly less likely results running down either side.

The idea is this: What's more useful to you as an investor—knowing that $100 invested monthly for 30 years at 10% annually is $227,932.53, or that, based on all the variables that historically have impacted the market, there's only a 50% chance that you'll actually reach that level? If you're comfortable with that risk, fine—so long as you realize that your portfolio may or may not achieve some level you assumed it would years ago based on an average-annual-return calculation. If you want a greater assurance of reaching that level, then maybe it makes sense to save a little more each month or change your asset mix to include riskier assets with the potential for greater reward.

Retirement income calculators run by T. Rowe Price (www.troweprice.com) and Financial Engines (www.financialengines.com), among others, rely on Monte Carlo analysis. T. Rowe Price's is free. Financial Engines charges a fee, though the information is more detailed.

tremendous amount of financial stress you might otherwise feel, providing an assured level of monthly cash flow to pay for life's necessities, freeing up Social Security and other sources of money to pay for health care or medicines or travel and leisure.

But before you invest in any annuity, understand what you're buying and why you're buying it, and make sure you're buying the right type of annuity for your needs.

All annuities are built around the same basic structure: they are hybrid investment/insurance contracts sold by insurance companies. For a sum of cash they generate a guaranteed monthly payment that can begin immediately or at some point in the future, and can last as few as five years or stretch over the remainder of your life span, what is known as the lifetime income option. There are all manner of ways to structure an annuity payout. You could, for instance, take the largest payout available for the number of years you think you'll need it, but if you die before the final payment, the insurer keeps your original investment and your heirs receive nothing. Or, you can arrange it so that the payouts are guaranteed to continue for a set number of years, going to your designated beneficiary if you expire before the payments do.

For people seeking income, an annuity will always provide more than a certificate of deposit, even if the size of the account and the returns are identical. That's because while a CD returns interest income, an annuity also returns a portion of the original principal you invested. The upshot of that: When the CD matures, you still have your original investment; when the annuity comes to an end, you'll have no remaining value in the account since you consumed it along the way. Of course, with a CD, you'll have to continually roll the money over into a new CD when the current one matures, and you never know if interest rates will be higher of lower the next time around, meaning your income could be lower than you need if rates fall sharply, as happened to many retirees in the 1990s and into the early 2000s. With an annuity, you can lock in your monthly income for fifteen or twenty years, or longer.

Variations on annuities are legion, and each has different bells and whistles that provide all sorts of additional benefits at additional costs. But essentially annuities break down into two major types—immediate and deferred.

With *immediate annuities*, you trade a one-time lump sum of cash for a recurring stream of income that begins immediately, or within the year. Once you buy an immediate annuity, you cannot retrieve that lump sum or the remaining portion of it if you decide you need the cash at some point. Instead, your money is returned to you over a predetermined period or the remainder of your life.

Deferred annuities, meanwhile, have two phases: the accumulation phase, in which your principal grows in value over many years, and a distribution phase, in which you can reclaim your money, plus all the earnings, through a one-time lump-sum payout or a monthly stream of income.

The biggest pitfall with deferred annuities is that most of them impose so-called surrender penalties, charges you must pay if you decide you want your money back before a certain amount of time has elapsed. That time is measured in years, usually somewhere between seven and ten years, though in some instances it can be much longer. The charges can be onerous, anywhere from 8% to 10%—or more—of the contract's value.

Both immediate and deferred annuities can be either fixed or variable.

A *fixed annuity* pays a fixed rate of return, just like a CD. The returns inside a *variable annuity* depend entirely upon the performance of the mutual-fund–like sub-accounts that you choose and which invest in everything from cash to stock and bonds.

WHICH ANNUITY IS RIGHT FOR ME?

Here's a very short quiz to answer that question:

Are you retired?

If "no" is your answer, then you want a variable annuity. While you're still in the workforce, your variable annuity will have many years to grow (a decade or two is best) during a period in which you don't need the money to live on. Then, at some point after you reach retirement, you can annuitize the account balance and create that guaranteed base of income to supplement whatever other income you have.

If "yes" is your answer, then you want an immediate annuity. Once you're in retirement, you're generally not as concerned about growing your assets as you are with generating enough income to live your life. That's precisely the roll of an immediate annuity—to generate income. A variable annuity tends to be a poor choice for retirees since retirees generally don't have the time necessary to let a variable annuity grow. That's particularly true of older retirees, those in their late seventies and eighties, who are often targets of unscrupulous annuity sellers. When you're older you almost assuredly do not want your money locked away from you for years at a time; you may need that cash for an emergency and you're going to hate having to pay a surrender charge to reclaim it.

Younger retirees who might want to assure a certain level of income in later years can get away with putting some money into a variable annuity, so long as it's a low-cost annuity such as the Lifetime Variable Select sold by New York retirement-services giant TIAA-CREF, the Vanguard Variable Annuity sold by the mutual fund company Vanguard Group in Malvern, Pennsylvania, or the Fidelity Personal Retirement Annuity sold by Boston's Fidelity Investments. Each of those annuities charges some of the lowest fees in the industry and none impose a surrender charge, meaning you can reclaim your money if necessary at any point without relinquishing a chunk of it to the insurer.

A TAXING MATTER

You must understand how the IRS will tax your annuity before you decide to buy one, since you could unwittingly and substantially increase the taxes you or your heirs owe the government.

Earnings from an annuity are taxed as ordinary income, which is usually a higher rate than the capital-gains rate at which stocks and mutual funds are taxed. Moreover, annuities receive no "step-up provision" (more on that in a moment), which can create a much larger tax obligation on heirs who might inherit an annuity you leave behind.

Here's how it all shakes out:

With an immediate annuity, the portion of your monthly payment that represents earnings is taxed as ordinary income. The portion that represents a return of your original principal is not taxed.

With deferred annuities, you pay no taxes on the earnings, if any, that accumulate each year. Like a 401(k) or IRA account, these annuities grow tax-deferred. However, you will pay taxes once you begin to draw on the money as either a lump sum or a monthly payout. And you'll pay at the higher ordinary-income rates.

Now, where deferred annuities really stab the unprepared is with that step-up provision. With stocks and mutual funds, the value of the asset at the time of your death becomes your heirs' cost basis. Meaning: If you own $100,000 worth of a mutual fund that originally cost you, say, $10,000, your heirs won't pay capital-gains taxes on the $90,000 in profits you amassed. For tax purposes, their clock starts running at $100,000.

With an annuity, however, heirs will pay taxes—at the higher ordinary-income rates—on all of the $90,000 in profits. For that reason, retirees in particular should be very leery of trading stocks and mutual funds in which they have big profits for an annuity. In doing so, you're creating taxes where none exist.

CONCLUSION

Really, was that so bad?

You made it to the end and survived all the math. And with a little effort you have taken the steps necessary to become a better steward of your money, and to invest with greater confidence in your own abilities to adequately allocate the assets in your 401(k) plan and IRA. You know a P/E ratio from your high school PE class and, more important, you know how to calculate it and several other Wall Street numbers.

You know how to determine what amount of life insurance you need to properly protect your assets and your family, you know how much money you need in your emergency savings account, how much you need to save each month to reach your retirement requirements, and why that 0% financing deal your car dealership is pitching isn't necessarily as rosy as it seems.

In short, you've become more self-sufficient with the money that flows through your life, and more capable in managing the finances of living for today while saving and investing for tomorrow.

But perhaps most important is, hopefully, the realization that personal finance is not such a difficult subject after all, and that you really do already have all the tools needed to succeed in the game of money. It's not scary. It's not hard. It can be empowering to take charge of your finances. And, sometimes, it can be fun.

Even if it does require a bit of math.

INDEX

accountability, 9
annuities, 164, 167–70
  deferred, 168, 169
  fixed, 168
  immediate, 167–68, 169
  lifetime income option, 167
  and retirement, 168–69
  step-up provision, 169–70
  surrender penalties of, 168
  and taxes, 169
  variable, 168–69
asset allocation, 118, 153–56
  age-based, 154, 155
  bond component in, 154, 155, 161
  for college savings, 91
  models, 154–55, 161
assets:
  building (investments), 117–43
  and college financial aid, 87
  equity in, 69
  and net worth, 118, 120; worksheet, 119
  personal inventory (worksheet), 54–56
Association for Financial Counseling, 63
auto insurance, 52, 100, 102; *see also* cars
average annual returns, 166

balance transfer credit cards, 67–68
banking, 35–48
  balance carried in, 35
  CDs, 40–45
  checking accounts, 36, 40; worksheets, 38–39, 41
  custodial accounts, 85
  fees for, 35–36
  linked accounts in, 36
  perks in, 36
  services (worksheet), 37
bonds:
  asset allocation, 154, 155, 161
  bond funds vs., 155
  index funds, 159
  rate of return (worksheet), 136
  ratings of, 154
  TIPS, 159
  U.S. savings, 23–24
  U.S. Treasury, 120–21
  yields of, 134
book value, 134
borrowing, 61–102
  cost of (money factor), 99
  see also debt
brokerage firms, 129–32
  commissions to, 130
  custodial accounts, 85
  deciding where to invest, 156
  discount, 131–32
  fees, 130
  full-service, 130–31

budgeting, 7–34
annual, 29–34; worksheet, 31–33
emergency savings in, 25–29
personal, 9–11; worksheet, 10–11
for savings, 22
and spending plans, 8, 12–20

capitalized cost, 99, 100
cars:
buying, 92–95
capitalized cost, 99, 100
comparing leases on, 100–102; worksheet, 101
insurance, 52, 100, 102
leasing, 95, 99; money factor chart, 98; worksheet, 97
lemon laws, 100
money factor turned into interest rate, 99
negotiations for, 100
purchase vs. finance (worksheet), 93–94
residual value, 99
zero financing, 95; worksheet, 96
cash:
debt vs., 61
irrevocable gifts of, 83
purchases with, 66–67
CDs (certificates of deposit), 40–45
basic principles of, 41
breaking, 45; worksheet, 42
compounded interest (chart), 43–44
early withdrawal penalty, 45
laddering, 47–48
rule of thumb with, 48
checking accounts, 36, 40
balancing a checkbook, 38–39
force balancing, 40; worksheet, 41
closing costs (house), 76, 78
college:
advanced placement, 91
and asset allocation, 91
costs of, 83
Coverdell accounts, 84, 85
custodial accounts, 83–85
financial aid, 81, 86, 87, 91
529 plans, 84, 85
how much to save for, 86–91; worksheet, 88–90
qualified education expenses, 86
saving for, 81, 83; chart, 84; worksheet, 88–90
work-study plans, 83
College Level Examination Program (CLEP) tests, 91
company stock, 162
compound interest, 127–28; charts, 43–44, 127
computers, vulnerability of data on, 113
Coverdell Education Savings Accounts, 84, 85
credit cards:
balance transfer, 67–68
canceling, 68
closing accounts, 68
limiting use of, 66–67
paying off, 66, 67–68
wallet register, 103–4; worksheet, 105
credit scores, 68
custodial accounts, 83–85

debt:
aggregate of, 65
attention paid to spending, 65–66
cash vs., 61
closing accounts, 68
cost of borrowing (money factor), 99
on credit cards, 66
determining the amount of, 64–65
paying down, 64–68
paying with cash, 66–67
too much, 62–64
total (worksheet), 65
debt-to-income ratio, 63; worksheet, 64
deferred annuities, 168
DirectInvesting.com, 141
discipline, 9
discount brokerage firms, 131–32
discretionary income, 8, 66
diversification, 139, 156, 160–61
dividend yield, 134
documents:
where to keep, 106, 111, 113; worksheet, 112

dollar-cost averaging, 140–41; worksheet, 142–43
DRiP (dividend reinvestment plan), 141; worksheet, 142–43
DSP (direct stock purchase plan), 141; worksheet, 142–43

effective tax rate, 79
emergency savings, 25–29, 128
  formula, 26
  worksheet, 27–28
equity, 69, 79–81
escrow account, 73
ETFs (exchange-traded funds), 139
expenses:
  discretionary, 30
  emergency (worksheet), 27–28
  estimate of, 30
  family-expense fund, 58
  fixed, 29
  and income, 8
  qualified education, 85; chart, 86

FAFSA (free application for federal student aid), 87
family documents, 111; worksheet, 112
family-expense fund, 58
family finance personal record (worksheet), 107–10
financial accounts, inventory, 104, 106
financial aid for college, 81, 86
  and FAFSA forms, 87
  scams, 87
  scholarships, 87, 91
Financial Engines, 166
Financial Planning Association, 63
529 college savings plans, 84, 85
fixed annuities, 168
401(k) plans:
  diversification in, 160
  options available in, 156, 158–60
  saving via, 23
full-service brokerage firms, 130–31

growth rate, 135

home:
  affordability of, 72–76; worksheet, 74
  buying, 68–69, 128–29
  cost of buying, 70, 76, 78
  equity in, 69, 79–81; worksheet, 80
  renting vs. buying, 69–72; chart, 70; worksheet, 71
  tax savings in, 78–79; chart, 79
home owner's insurance, 52–53
  and land value, 52
  property inventory for, 53; worksheet, 54–56

immediate annuities, 167–68, 169
income:
  debt-to-income ratio, 63; worksheet, 64
  discretionary, 8, 66
  estimate of, 29
  and expenses, 8
  spending over, 9
index investing, 138–39, 158, 159
inflation, 46
insurance, 49–60
  auto, 52, 100, 102
  home owner's, 52–53
  life, *see* life insurance
  private mortgage (PMI), 80–81
  shopping for, 59; worksheet, 60
  value of, 50
interest rates:
  compounded (chart), 43–44
  and laddering, 47–48
  and money factor, 99
  mortgage (chart), 75
international stocks, 158–59
inventory:
  financial accounts, 104, 106; worksheets, 107–10
  key family documents, 111; worksheet, 112
  personal property, 53
  videotaped, 53
  wallet register, 103–4; worksheet, 105
  worksheet, 54–56
investments, 117–43
  annuities, 164, 167–70
  asset allocation, 153–56, 161
  average annual returns, 166

investments (*cont.*):
book value of, 134
buy-and-hold, 139
compounded interest in, 127–28; chart, 127
deciding where to invest, 156–60
diversification of, 139, 156, 160–61
dollar-cost averaging, 140–41
foundation of, 128
goal of, 137
indexed, 138–39, 159
IRAs, 162–64; chart, 165
laddering, 47–48
lifecycle funds, 160
market capitalization, 138
Monte Carlo models, 166
net profit margin, 133–34
P/E ratio, 132–33
rate of return, 135–38; worksheet, 136–37
REITs, 159
required minimum distribution, 164
risk tolerance in, 120–22, 162; worksheet, 123–25
sector funds, 159–60
time frames for, 126; chart, 126
see also bonds; stock
IRAs, 162–64
chart, 165
deciding where to invest, 156, 160
education, 85
required minimum distribution, 164
irrevocable gifts, 83

laddering your investments, 47–48
land value, and insurance, 52
large-cap companies, 138
lifecycle funds, 160
life insurance:
and family-expense fund, 58
how much coverage in, 53, 57; worksheet, 58–59
income replacement, 57
who needs it, 50; chart, 51

marginal tax rate, 79
market capitalization, 138
micro-cap companies, 138
mid-cap companies, 138
money:
control of, 8, 34
thinking about, 8
money factor, chart, 98; and interest rate, 99
Monte Carlo models, 166
Morningstar, 135, 156–57, 158, 160
mortgage:
back-end ratio, 73
closing costs, 76, 78
in escrow account, 73
front-end ratio for, 72–73
and home buying, 68–69
and insurance, 53
interest rates and term (chart), 75
lender formulas for, 72
as lien, 68
PITI (principal, interest, taxes, insurance) in, 73
PMI, 80–81
points, 76
refinancing, 81; worksheet, 82
shopping for, 76–78; worksheet, 77
tax deduction for, 69
mutual funds, 118
custodial accounts, 85
in diversified investment, 160–61
dollar-cost averaging, 141
exchange-traded (ETF), 139
market capitalization, 138
picking, 157
rate of return (worksheet), 136–37

National Association of Personal Financial Advisors, 63
net asset value (NAV), 137
net profit margin, 133–34
net worth, calculating, 118, 120; worksheet, 119

PEG ratio, 135
penny stocks, 138
P/E ratio (price-to-earning ratio), 132–33
Pink Sheets, trading on, 138

PITI (principal, interest, taxes, insurance), 73
PMI (private mortgage insurance), 80–81
points (mortgage), 76

qualified education expenses, 85; chart, 86

rate of return, calculating, 135–38; worksheet, 136–37
REITs (real estate investment trusts), 159
required minimum distribution, 164
residual value, 99
retirement, 145–70
  and annuities, 168–69
  costs (worksheet), 147–52
  how much you'll need for, 145–53
  income calculators for, 166
  income-replacement rule of thumb, 146
  participation in employer's plan (chart), 163
  as priority in savings plan, 83, 128
  tax-advantaged accounts, 162–64
risk:
  and Monte Carlo models, 166
  tolerance for, 120–22, 162; worksheet, 123–25
  use of term, 120
Roth IRA, 165
Russell 2000 index fund, 158

S&P 500 Index fund, 158
safe-deposit boxes, 106, 111, 113
savings:
  automatic, 23
  for college, *see* college
  emergency, 25–29, 128
  paying yourself first, 20–24
  rule of thumb for, 22
  strategies for, 23–24
  and wealth, 24
  worksheet, 22
scholarships, 81
  merit, 87
  sources of, 87
  state-funded, 87, 91
sector funds, 159–60
SEP IRA, 165
small-cap companies, 138, 158
spending plans, 8, 12–20
  adjusting, 13
  and annual budget, 30
  finding missing money in, 20
  flexibility in, 21
  interacting with, 13
  major events affecting, 21
  monthly balance, 19–20; worksheet, 19
  negative numbers in, 20
  paying yourself first, 20–24
  projections in, 12
  value of, 19
  worksheet, 14–19
step-up provision, 169–70
stock:
  asset allocation, 154, 155, 161
  book value of, 134
  company, 162
  direct purchase plan, 141; worksheet, 142–43
  index investing, 138–39, 158
  international, 158–59
  and PEG ratio, 135
  penny, 138
  P/E ratio, 132–33
  Pink Sheet trades of, 138
  rate of return (worksheet), 136
  yield of, 134
surrender penalties, 168

TIPS (Treasury Inflation-Protected Securities), 159
Treasury bonds, 120–21
T. Rowe Price, 166

UGMA and UTMA accounts, 83–85
U.S. savings bonds, 23–24
U.S. Treasury bonds, 120–21

variable annuities, 168–69
vocabulary, 132–33

wallet register, 103–4; worksheet, 105
wealth, and savings, 24
worksheets:
  affordable housing, 74
  annual budget, 31–33
  auto lease comparison, 101
  balancing a checkbook, 38
  bank services, 37
  breaking a CD, 42
  car buying vs. financing, 93–94
  car buying vs. leasing, 97
  checking account, 38–39, 41
  college cost and savings calculator, 88–90
  debt-to-income ratio, 64
  dollar-cost averaging, 142–43
  emergency expenses, 27–28
  family documents, 112
  family finance personal record, 107–10
  force balancing a checkbook, 41
  home buying vs. renting, 71
  home equity, 80
  how much life insurance to buy, 58–59
  monthly balance, 19
  net worth, 119
  personal budget, 10–11
  personal property inventory, 54–56
  rate of return, 136–37
  refinancing a mortgage, 82
  retirement costs, 147–52
  risk tolerance, 123–25
  savings, 22
  shopping for insurance, 60
  shopping for a mortgage, 77
  spending plan, 14–19
  total debt, 65
  wallet register, 105
  zero financing, 96
work-study plans, 83

Yahoo! Finance, 158
yield, meaning of term, 134

zero financing, 95; worksheet, 96

ABOUT THE AUTHOR

JEFF D. OPDYKE is a financial reporter who has covered investing and personal finance for *The Wall Street Journal* for the past twelve years. He is also a columnist for *The Wall Street Journal* Sunday supplement, writing the Love & Money column that is syndicated in roughly ninety papers nationwide and which explores the nexus of personal finance and personal relationships. Opdyke is the author of *Love & Money: The Life Guide to Financial Success.* Prior to joining the *Journal* in 1993, Opdyke was a staff writer for the *Orange County Register* in Southern California and the *Fort Worth* (Tex.) *Star-Telegram.* He spent a nine-month sabbatical as an analyst and trader for a Dallas-based hedge fund. Opdyke is a graduate of the Louisiana State University Manship School of Journalism. He lives in Baton Rouge, Louisiana, with his wife, Amy, and their two children.